SETTING THE STANDARD
for HEALTHFUL, GRAIN-FREE COOKING

Beloved for stunning and clean-yet-decadent cakes and confections, the grain-free brand Sweet Laurel offers its most delightful savory provisions, from pantry staples and breads to pastas, pizzas, and feasts. The recipes are gluten-free and refined sugar–free with keto, paleo, dairy-free, and vegan options, as well. Whether you're working toward a more wholesome way of eating and living or working around food allergies, *Sweet Laurel Savory* brings satisfying simplicity to breakfast, lunch, dinner, and beyond.

   With Sweet Laurel's uncomplicated whole-food approach, the recipes here are as doable as they are flavorful and healthy. Simple and readily available core ingredients build the foundation for indulgent favorites and craveable staples. With options like **Sicilian Pan Pizza**, **Epic Bagel Spread**, **The Ultimate Sweet Laurel Burger with Sweet Potato Fries**, and **Zucchini Lattice Tart**, you'll never feel restricted.

SWEET

SWEET LAUREL *savory*

EVERYDAY DECADENCE
FOR WHOLE-FOOD, GRAIN-FREE MEALS

LAUREL GALLUCCI & CLAIRE THOMAS

Clarkson Potter/Publishers
New York

With love to our eternally
tolerant husbands, Nick and Craig

CONTENTS

At Sweet Laurel, we might be best known for our decadent grain-free layer cakes, cinnamon-dusted snickerdoodles, or double-chocolate brownies. But when we've frosted our last jam cake of the day, our minds turn to dinner, just like any other home cook. Well, not *just* dinner. Though our sweet tooth is mighty, we love the savory just as much: brunch, lunch, breads, salads, pizzas, dips, platters—anything you find bouncing around between the cookie crumbs. Just as we believe everyone should be able to have a slice of cake on their birthday, no matter their journey or challenges with food, we also believe everyone should be able to enjoy pancakes in bed or a fun Taco Tuesday.

So many who have found Sweet Laurel have come to us because they feel a connection to our personal struggle with chronic health conditions. It's easy to feel alone in the struggle to understand your body and what it needs, or like you have to put your life on hold to accommodate those needs, but Sweet Laurel is and has always been about the freedom and ability to enjoy everyday decadence.

In 2012, Laurel was diagnosed with Hashimoto's disease, an autoimmune condition that affects the thyroid. In Laurel's case, her digestive system, hormone levels, and energy were catastrophically affected. She couldn't eat without experiencing severe stomach pain, she could barely climb a flight of stairs, and she was told she may never have children. She was ready for a change. When Laurel's doctor told her to remove all grains, gluten, refined sugar, soy, legumes, and dairy from her diet to adhere to a strict paleo protocol, she had the same question most people ask: *Well, what* can *I eat, then?*

When she began to do research, she discovered the many magical superfoods that have power to heal, as well as add to everyday deliciousness. She began what she calls her "healing through food" protocol. Being on such a strict diet meant Laurel cooked most of her

1

meals at home, and living within that scenario, she became very well versed in what it looks like to have a kitchen free of gluten, grains, refined sugar, and dairy.

After a few months, Laurel began to develop recipes for things she missed the most—at first it was mainly cakes, cookies, and brownies. Then came tea sandwiches, crostini, sweet potato rolls, and finally pizza and bread. With these nourishing wholesome recipes, Laurel began to heal.

Meanwhile, Claire's body can easily tolerate dairy, grains, and pretty much anything else, yet she still adores Sweet Laurel food. Of course, we have a large base that follows a strict diet that eliminates wheat, dairy, corn, soy, refined sugar, gums, and/or fillers. We are sometimes surprised to hear that our customers can tolerate gluten and grains just fine, but they're searching for options that are less inflammatory and generally healthier. For some, our food is a solution, and for others, it's just wholesome and nutritious. One of the most rewarding parts of this journey has been facing these food restrictions by using creativity to build more inclusive food practices with a simple approach—one that never equates to sacrifice.

A few years later, Laurel's autoimmune disease is in complete remission—and we have not one but two cookbooks to share with you.

ABOUT THIS BOOK

This book contains multitudes of healthy and delicious foods, along with adaptable practices for becoming a daily cook and baker. Grain-free baking is broken down and more approachable than ever.

We start with basic, core baking recipes, which are the foundation for the meals you'll find later in the book. We then cover the meals you can make with our baking recipes, plus a few recipes to pair with our baked goods. From weeknight favorites to celebratory holiday entrées, comfort foods to chic brunch buffet spreads—our hope is that your home-cooked discoveries will fill the needs of your hearts and homes and inform your cooking and baking for years to come.

We've gone through our families' recipes scrawled on index cards, unearthed our personal stashes of vintage cookbooks, and recalled our favorite meals we grew up eating. This cookbook is a deeply personal extension of our first cookbook and of the Sweet Laurel brand. Each recipe is meant to be accessible, delicious, and crowd-pleasing. You can enjoy this food at a fancy brunch with friends or on the couch with your partner. We hope you love these recipes as much as we do.

ABOUT OUR RECIPES

In developing recipes, our goal is always to honor our precious food memories by building on them and aligning them with what our bodies can tolerate.

Laurel's top priority is always ingredient quality. She is Sweet Laurel's resident health nerd and is deep into her journey of healing through food. Ensuring that each recipe is both flavorful and free of anything unnatural is essential, as this is the type of food that has helped heal her body. Laurel handpicks every ingredient we work with at Sweet Laurel to make sure it measures up to quality and health standards.

Claire is a purist, so her touch is apparent in the integrity of the final product. Pasta should taste like pasta, pizza should taste like pizza, and so on. Her dedication to tinkering and tweaking recipes until they taste just right is what gave us our reputation.

The combination of these two philosophies means each recipe has a healing, good-for-you component, while also tasting like the real thing—or perhaps an even better version of the real thing.

Our motto at Sweet Laurel has always been to keep it simple. Whether we're turning an elaborate chocolate layer cake recipe into a simple cake with even simpler frosting or taking on the challenge of making a grain-free brioche, this approach stays the same. That's because we believe in giving yourself the ability to feed your family and yourself daily. All our recipes are grain-free, refined-sugar-free, and dairy-free (no milk solids). We don't use legumes or gums. Our recipes all adhere to Laurel's anti-inflammatory diet, which she followed during her battle with Hashimoto's disease, now in remission. Our focus is on creating the most delicious recipes, using as few ingredients as possible.

Here is a key to some symbols you will see next to certain recipes:

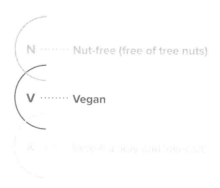

N ········ Nut-free (free of tree nuts)

V ········ Vegan

OUR SAVORY KITCHEN

FIVE CORE INGREDIENTS

Sweet Laurel's philosophy revolves around five core ingredients because we believe in simplicity, approachability, and value. With sweet baking, our goal is for soft, tender, smooth, and aerated textures, but with our savory recipes, we want chew, crunch, and snap. We use a lot of the same ingredients in both scenarios, but we combine them in different ways to achieve our desired texture.

Cassava Flour

Cassava is a lightweight, dusty flour that loves liquids. It has a subtle nutty flavor, so it's particularly good in savory recipes with bold flavors. However, in loaves, it can lead to a crusty outside and gummy, underdone middle, so we always combine it with another gluten-free flour to get a consistent bake.

Of all the grain-free flours we use, cassava behaves the most like conventional wheat flour. This means it binds together and has good structure all on its own, and can oftentimes even be swapped one-to-one with wheat flour.

Be careful not to mix it up with tapioca flour, though! Cassava flour and tapioca flour come from the same root, but are very different ingredients. Cassava is the tuberous root of a woody shrub native to South America. Cassava is produced from the entire root, peeled, dried, and ground. To make tapioca flour, the root is washed, pulped, and then squeezed to extract a starchy liquid. Once all the liquid evaporates, what remains is the tapioca flour.

Almond Flour

Almond flour is typically made from almonds that have been blanched. It's a nutritionally dense flour: compared to other tree nuts, almonds are higher in fiber, calcium, vitamin E, riboflavin, and niacin—plus, they are low-glycemic and offer other nutrients like magnesium. One ounce of almonds provides 6 grams of protein, 4 grams of fiber, and 14 grams of fat, two-thirds of which is heart-healthy monounsaturated fat.

If you are allergic to almonds, you can substitute hazelnut flour or cashew flour in our recipes. If you're allergic to hazelnuts and cashews as well, you can usually substitute coconut flour, with some additional adjustments (see Tip, page 14).

Arrowroot Powder/Starch

Arrowroot powder is a neutral-tasting thickener made from the arrowroot plant. It serves a purpose similar to cornstarch but is much less inflammatory. Arrowroot is a great alternative to cornstarch when you want to make things crunchy or crispy. If you're planning to substitute it for cornstarch, it's best to use one-third or half the amount of cornstarch called for. Not only do we use it as a binder in our baked goods, but we also use it to thicken sauces and soups. It helps add a chewy texture to our flatbreads and loaves that makes them perfect for building sandwiches. Arrowroot also helps lighten the texture of our breads. It has become a favorite ingredient to use with almond flour to reduce density, which is a common complaint about grain-free breads.

Eggs

We believe in using organic eggs from happy chickens. Eggs are an excellent source of choline and selenium, and a good source of high-quality protein, vitamin D, vitamin B_{12}, phosphorus, and riboflavin. They contain omega-3 fatty acids, which are essential to your diet. In baking, eggs are an indispensable binder, bringing ingredients together; a leavening agent, creating lift and lightness in texture; and, important for us, protein, which provides structure in our gluten-free recipes.

We also subscribe to the notion that almost any savory recipe is made better by putting an egg on it, like our burger (see page 189), Polenta Board (page 252), and, of course, egg toast on our Perfect Sandwich Bread (page 56). In most of our recipes, organic eggs can be replaced with any of our vegan egg recipes (see page 27).

Himalayan Pink Salt

Himalayan pink salt is not only beautiful to look at, but it is also loaded with minerals—eighty-four of them, to be exact. Plus, it has pH-balancing qualities and it doesn't contain any bleach or anticaking agents. Many people ask if using pink salt adds a different flavor or color to your finished product; the answer is no and no. We believe Himalayan pink salt naturally enhances flavor thanks to its high quality—that's the main reason we love it so much. If you do not have Himalayan pink salt, we recommend using sea salt as an alternative.

OTHER INGREDIENTS

Yeast

Sometimes yeast can feel like a wild animal—and with good reason! Essentially, yeast is a one-celled organism that feeds on sugar and water to create carbon dioxide, which is what makes yeasted breads rise. If the yeast doesn't have anything to eat, it won't rise; if the temperature is too cold, it'll be sleepy; and if the temperature is too hot, it dies.

We use active dry yeast in all our recipes. This type needs to proof in liquid before being used, unlike instant yeast, which is added directly to the dry ingredients. When you combine active dry yeast with liquid, it should look puffy and foamy within 10 minutes. If it doesn't, either the liquid was too hot or the yeast is dead; in either case, you'll need to start over with new yeast.

Yeast reacts differently in grain-free recipes than it does with conventional wheat flour. In wheat- or grain-based recipes, you'll commonly see dough double in size within a few hours, whereas with grain-free doughs, you'll see just a slight puff. The yeast adds a lighter, fluffier interior and that delicious freshly baked flavor.

Coconut Flour

Coconut flour is lower in fat and much drier than almond flour but still contains many nutrients, including vitamins C, E, B_1, B_3, B_5, and B_6, plus lots of fiber. You'll notice that our recipes with coconut flour have many wet ingredients to balance out the fiber, which means coconut flour is not a one-to-one replacement for almond or any other flour. If you're substituting in coconut flour, see the tip.

> Tip: Coconut flour soaks up liquid almost too efficiently, so if you need to replace nut flour with coconut flour, you need to also add liquid. Our basic equation is to replace 1 cup nut flour with ¼ cup coconut flour plus an additional egg. If the recipe does not contain any eggs, it's best not to substitute the coconut flour.

Tapioca Flour/Starch

Tapioca flour behaves similarly to cornstarch. It works as a great thickener in sauces, soups, and some of our breads, adding a bouncy and gooey texture.

Many folks ask us if tapioca is interchangeable with arrowroot, and the answer is mostly yes. It has a neutral flavor and works brilliantly as a thickener, just like arrowroot. It's naturally sticky and chewy, helping doughs bind together. The main difference, and why we tend to use arrowroot more often than tapioca, is that tapioca can get rubbery if you use too much of it. We tend to use tapioca in flatbreads where we want a bit of chew and stretch.

Baking Powder

We make our own baking powder (see page 28) because the store-bought stuff typically contains cornstarch and aluminum. It's an easy recipe and totally worth taking the extra care to avoid unnatural ingredients.

For dry ingredients, fluff the dry ingredient by scooping it with a measuring cup and then pouring it back into its container, or use a fork to fluff it five or six times. Then scoop the measuring cup in deeply and use a knife or your finger to swipe across the top to get an even level. Do not slam the measuring cup on the counter or press the dry ingredients down to pack the measuring cup.

For wet ingredients, always use a liquid measuring cup—it does make a difference.

When baking powder is moistened in a dough or batter, a chemical reaction takes place that produces carbon dioxide gas, inflating cookies, cakes, and pancakes. Because baking powder combines both an acid and a base, it eliminates the need for ingredients like buttermilk or sour cream.

Baking powder just regulates how air cells expand—whether a dough can *handle* that expansion depends on gluten. Recipes that are relatively acidic, lean, low in sugar, and high in moisture foster gluten development. Recipes that are relatively alkaline, rich, high in sugar, and low in moisture don't. In our recipes, baking powder is used mostly as a raising agent to encourage a rise where the gluten isn't present like in traditional breads.

Too much baking powder can cause a batter to taste bitter. It can also cause the batter to rise rapidly and then collapse, because the air bubbles grow too large and break, causing the batter to fall. Too little baking powder results in a tough texture with poor volume and a compact crumb.

WHEN TO USE WHICH FLOUR

Our recipes are carefully calibrated for the ingredients in them, and they all react very differently. We urge you not to swap flours in our recipes, but here's a quick reference guide to explain our choices.

Almond Flour: Moist and oily, it gives breads a soft and cakey crumb.

Cassava Flour: The most similar to wheat flour, cassava acts as a great binder without getting gummy, but it can be a bit heavy. It has a slightly nutty aftertaste.

Arrowroot and Tapioca Flours: Both of these flours are quite starchy and provide the same benefits as cornstarch, so we use these for binding and smoothing things together. Be careful not to use too much, or you can get a gummy consistency. They are also quite heavy and can weigh down recipes if too much is added.

Coconut Flour: Extremely fibrous, this flour adds excellent structure but requires a ton of liquid. Add too little liquid, and you'll end up with something extremely dense and tough.

Baking Soda

We use natural baking soda, meaning baking soda that has been mined rather than lab-created.

Baking soda, also known as sodium bicarbonate, is about four times as strong as baking powder. It is used in recipes that contain an acidic ingredient, like vinegar, citrus juice, sour cream, yogurt, chocolate, honey, fruits, and maple syrup, and being alkaline, the baking soda counteracts them. It starts to react and release carbon dioxide gas as soon as it is added to the batter and moistened. Make sure to bake the batter immediately.

Baking soda has an indefinite shelf life if stored in an airtight container in a cool, dry place. Using too much of it in a recipe will result in a soapy taste with a coarse, bubbly crumb.

> Tip: Since baking soda works with foods that are acidic, if you are making biscuits that call for buttermilk and baking soda and you substitute with nut milk, your biscuits may not rise because the acidic element isn't present. Simply add 1 tablespoon vinegar to each cup of nut milk to correct this.

Cider Vinegar

Cider vinegar is fermented apple juice, and we like to use it in recipes needing extra brightness and lift. The acid in the vinegar adds a light texture and creates a sourdough tang. Fermented ingredients like this one were a huge part of Laurel's gut health recovery after her diagnosis; the acid in cider vinegar has the ability to kill dangerous "bad" bacteria and at the same time foster the growth of beneficial "good" bacteria. Look for raw, cold-pressed brands that have sediment at the bottom of the bottle, like Bragg.

Coconut Aminos

Coconut aminos is a staple in the grain-free and legume-free pantry. It typically replaces soy sauce, which is made with fermented soy and grains and usually contains wheat. Coconut aminos is made with just coconut tree sap and salt. It mimics the flavor profile of soy sauce almost exactly.

Grass-Fed Ghee

Ghee is a fantastic ingredient for adding richness and texture. Ghee is made by slowly melting butter to separate the butterfat from the milk solids, which are then discarded, rendering it lactose and casein-free. We choose grass-fed over conventional ghee, as it contains vitamin K, which is stellar for heart health, and 25 percent medium- and short-chain fatty acids, much like the fat found in coconut milk, which your body metabolizes faster and more easily than butter. For a vegan alternative, coconut oil is usually a suitable replacement. We use it both melted and chilled solid, depending on the recipe.

Coconut Oil and Milk

Coconut is one of the main foods Laurel used to build her body back up after being diagnosed with Hashimoto's disease. We love coconuts for their nutritional properties, delicious flavor, and versatility in a dairy-free kitchen. They are rich in fiber, vitamins C, E, B_1, B_3, B_5, and B_6, and minerals, but what we love most about coconuts is their fat. Most of the fat in coconut is made up of medium-chain saturated fatty acids, which are rapidly metabolized into energy in the liver and are less likely to be stored as fat in the body. Additionally, coconut oil can be heated to a very high temperature without losing its nutritional benefits, making it ideal for baking.

However, having a low melting point means that coconut oil is not the best choice for recipes that require chilled fat, such as pastry dough (see page 33). For a milder coconut flavor, use refined coconut oil.

We also use coconut milk in several of our recipes. Be sure to purchase coconut milk without additives that is packaged in BPA-free cans. Our favorite brand is Natural Value organic coconut milk.

Coconut Butter

Coconut butter, also known as coconut manna, is made from grinding dried coconut meat together. The difference between coconut butter and coconut oil is similar to that between peanut butter and peanut oil—one is a thick paste; the other is pure fat. Coconut butter is an excellent thickener and binder in recipes.

Avocado Oil

For dishes that are sautéed or fried and in any sauces, we like using avocado oil for its neutral taste. Avocado oil is high in oleic acid, monounsaturated fats, and vitamins A, E, and D; it also contains good amounts of magnesium and antioxidants, which most people do not consume enough of. Refined avocado oil has the highest smoke point of all oils available on the market. Avocado oil can serve as a substitute in most of our recipes that call for liquid coconut oil.

Nuts and Nut Butters

Nuts and nut butters can be powerful stand-ins for grains. They add structure and moisture and can be used as a base in breads and baked goods. Nuts are loaded with good fats and protein and, compared to grains, contain far fewer carbohydrates. Our first choice in most recipes is almond butter; however, hazelnut and cashew butters work beautifully, too. We love these options because they are widely available but also easy to make yourself (see page 27). If you're allergic to nuts, sunflower seed butter is a wonderful option.

Flax

Flaxseeds add a binding effect to baked goods when ground and added to liquid. We use them mixed with water as "vegan eggs" (see page 27) but also love the delicious flavor and texture they add to our rustic breads, like Perfect Sandwich Bread (page 56) and Sweet and Savory Honey "Corn Bread" (page 63). The additional benefit is that they're high in fiber and omega-3 fatty acids, as well as phytochemicals called lignans, which can help the body fight chronic illness and disease. If you can, grind them fresh for the best binding.

Chia

Chia seeds are similar to flaxseeds in that they're also full of omega-3 fatty acids and fiber and make a great egg substitute. When they're ground and combined with water, their fat and fiber will thicken even more than flax to create a gooey binding ingredient perfect for using in cakes and breads with a soft crumb and moist texture.

OUR FAVORITE KITCHEN TOOLS

Bowl and Whisk

We believe baking should be simple and essential, so most of the recipes in this book can be made with just a bowl and a whisk. We recommend always using a bowl larger than you think you need—it gives you more room to work and allows you to be more flexible with your movement.

Rolling Pin

To get perfectly thin layers, a rolling pin can't be beat. As much as we love a press-in crust, some recipes call for more precise thickness. It sounds like a little thing, but having an even thickness is what creates a smooth, golden brown bake versus an inconsistent, spotty, burnt-on-the-outside/soft-in-the-middle one.

Parchment Paper

Grain-free dough can be sticky. This may be because alternative flours require a lot of moisture or because of the fat in nut flours or the texture of arrowroot and tapioca flours. So rolling out a dough or baking it in a pan requires a little extra insurance. We use parchment paper to create a nonstick work surface as well as an easy way to transport loaves in and out of pans.

Zip-Top Bags

A zip-top bag makes the perfect last-minute piping bag. We like to use these bags for doughs in which egg whites have been folded in, like the dough for our oyster crackers (see page 93). Of course, if you have actual piping bags, those work great, too.

Pastry Brush

We frequently add a simple egg wash before baking to create golden brown, caramelized crusts, which are not only pretty to look at but delicious, too. A pastry brush is key to applying a thin, even layer of egg wash to your dough before it goes into the oven.

Rubber Spatula

We use the folding technique to get a light, bubbly texture in a lot of recipes. Folding is when you use a rubber spatula to roll the dough, batter, or mixture from around the sides of the bowl, then up and over, in one smooth movement. This allows you to keep as much air as possible while also incorporating other ingredients.

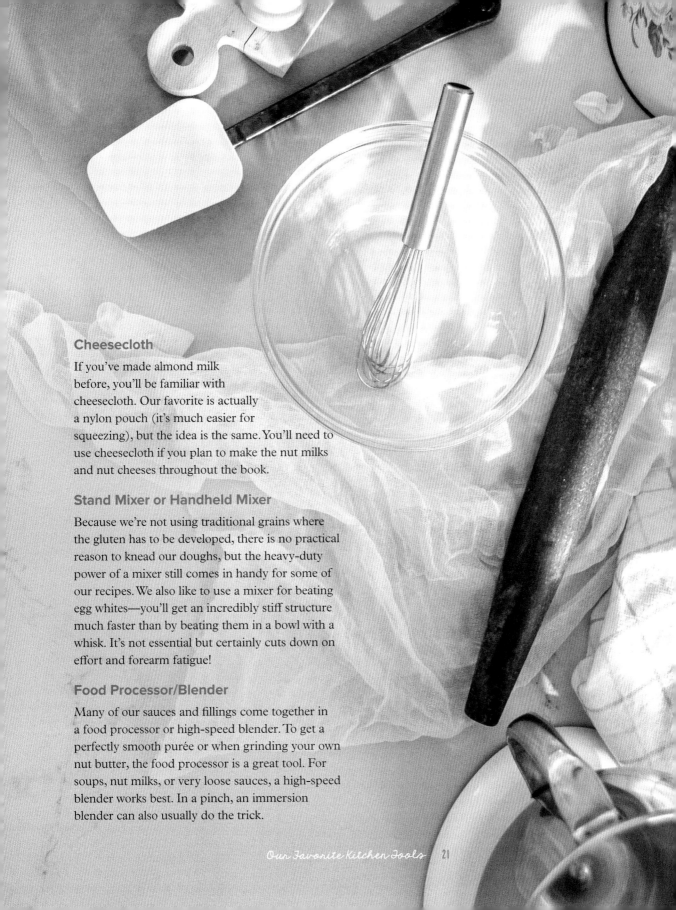

Cheesecloth

If you've made almond milk
before, you'll be familiar with
cheesecloth. Our favorite is actually
a nylon pouch (it's much easier for
squeezing), but the idea is the same. You'll need to
use cheesecloth if you plan to make the nut milks
and nut cheeses throughout the book.

Stand Mixer or Handheld Mixer

Because we're not using traditional grains where
the gluten has to be developed, there is no practical
reason to knead our doughs, but the heavy-duty
power of a mixer still comes in handy for some of
our recipes. We also like to use a mixer for beating
egg whites—you'll get an incredibly stiff structure
much faster than by beating them in a bowl with a
whisk. It's not essential but certainly cuts down on
effort and forearm fatigue!

Food Processor/Blender

Many of our sauces and fillings come together in
a food processor or high-speed blender. To get a
perfectly smooth purée or when grinding your own
nut butter, the food processor is a great tool. For
soups, nut milks, or very loose sauces, a high-speed
blender works best. In a pinch, an immersion
blender can also usually do the trick.

part one

PANTRY

"Puttin' up" is one of our favorite food sayings. If you're from the south, you're probably familiar with it. The act of "puttin' up" is filling your pantry with homemade preserves, part of the culture of thriftiness from a time past. When Laurel began her healing foods protocol, many of today's convenience items (such as dairy-free yogurt, clean nut milk, grain-free flours, etc.) weren't yet on the market, so she had to create her own at home. Luckily, Laurel was up to the task and created simple, delicious staples that are perfect for every pantry.

ALMOND MILK

Makes 4 cups

Almond milk is an essential ingredient at Sweet Laurel, and we've been making our own since day one. Once you get the hang of a nut milk bag or cheesecloth and make your own at home, you won't be able to stop. Homemade tastes so much better—creamy, rich, and pure. You will find almond milk called for in several of our recipes, but don't forget about the other perks of having homemade almond milk in your fridge. A splash in your coffee, smoothie, or in our Raisin Crunch Cereal (page 119) will make you a believer!

4 cups raw almonds

Himalayan pink salt

1 tablespoon raw honey or pure maple syrup (optional)

1. Place the almonds in a large bowl and add water to cover completely. Refrigerate for at least 8 hours.

2. Drain the almonds and transfer half to a blender. Add 5 cups cold water and a pinch of salt. Blend on high for about 2 minutes, until the mixture starts to look creamy. Transfer the mixture to a large bowl and repeat with the remaining whole almonds, 5 more cups cold water, and another pinch of salt.

3. Strain the mixture through cheesecloth or a nut milk bag into a large bowl, squeezing the cheesecloth or bag to extract the almond milk. Sweeten with honey, if using. Transfer to a jar and tightly seal the lid. Store in the fridge for up to 5 days. The almond pulp can be dehydrated and used as almond flour (though we recommend combining it with 50 percent regular almond flour to get the best results, as dehydrated almond pulp is drier than regular almond flour).

COCONUT YOGURT

Makes about 3½ cups

Coconut yogurt, which we've dubbed Coco Yo, is made primarily from coconut milk, a nutrient powerhouse that's full of good fats, particularly MCTs, a type of fat your body can metabolize quickly. This yogurt is fermented with a probiotic, adding richness to the gut flora. We use coconut yogurt in several of our recipes, and it is also excellent as a breakfast or healthy snack on its own.

2 (13.5-ounce) cans full-fat coconut milk, refrigerated overnight

2 probiotic capsules

½ teaspoon pure vanilla extract (optional)

1. Open the chilled cans of coconut milk and scoop the solid coconut cream that has risen to the top into a large glass jar with a tight-fitting lid. We like to use the leftover coconut liquid from the can in our smoothies. Stir in the probiotic capsules and vanilla (if using).

2. Place the jar in a dehydrator set to 110°F or in a turned-off oven, with the light on, for 12 to 18 hours, until the coconut appears slightly thickened and has a tart scent.

3. Store the yogurt in the fridge for up to 4 days.

NUT BUTTER

Makes 1½ cups

Nut butter is a versatile base for many of our recipes. Typically made with roasted almonds, it provides a smooth texture and stability in both baked goods and sauces alike. The lovely thing about this recipe is you can use any nut in place of the almonds to cater to any palate. Cashew, walnut, pecan, and pistachio all work great!

3 cups **almonds** or **nuts of your choice**

1. Preheat the oven to 400°F.

2. Spread the almonds over a baking sheet in a single layer. Roast for about 7 minutes, until fragrant and lightly browned.

3. Transfer the almonds to a food processor and process for about 3 minutes, stopping to scrape down the sides with a rubber spatula occasionally. The almond butter is ready when it is smooth and creamy—this takes about 5 to 10 minutes, so be patient!

4. Transfer the almond butter to a glass jar with a tight-fitting lid, seal, and store in the fridge for up to 3 weeks.

VEGAN EGGS

The three plant-based alternatives below mimic the structure of an egg, act as a binder, and add flavor. Vegan eggs can work as a replacement in most recipes but not all. Recipes that call for whipped egg white, for instance, require lift and aeration you can't get from vegan eggs. For any recipes using a vegan egg, add an extra 5 minutes in the oven. Each of the following mixtures will replace 1 egg. For any of these replacements, add them when the recipe calls for adding a regular egg.

- Mix together 1 part ground flax meal (also called ground flaxseed) and 3 parts hot water. Refrigerate for 15 minutes before using and use within the hour.

- Mix together 1 part ground chia seed and 3 parts hot water. Refrigerate for 5 minutes before using.

- Mix together 1 part psyllium husk and 4 parts hot water. Use immediately.

BAKING POWDER

······························· *Makes ³/₄ cup*

When we first discovered that some conventional baking powder brands contain aluminum and other inflammatory binders, we were determined to create our own. We quickly discovered how easy it is to mix together with just a few ingredients!

½ cup **cream of tartar**

¼ cup **baking soda**

Sift together the cream of tartar and the baking soda into a small jar. Tightly secure the lid and store in a cool dry place.

DIJON MUSTARD

······························· *Makes about ¹/₂ cup*

Bright, peppery, and the perfect secret ingredient, mustard adds wonderful lift to any recipe. However, Dijon mustard contains white wine, which Laurel doesn't consume, so we created our own Dijon to use in our recipes. It's simple to put together and will be a delicious addition to your pantry.

¼ cup **yellow mustard seeds**

2 tablespoons **brown mustard seeds**

1 tablespoon **mustard powder**

¼ cup **fresh lemon juice**

½ teaspoon **Himalayan pink salt**

1. Place the mustard seeds in a jar and add enough water to just cover the seeds. Set aside to soak overnight.

2. Transfer the seeds and their soaking liquid to a blender or food processor and add the mustard powder, lemon juice, and salt. Blend until smooth, about 1 minute, or longer if you prefer a more finely ground mustard.

3. Transfer to a clean glass jar, seal, and store in the fridge for up to 2 weeks.

SIMPLE MAYONNAISE

Makes 1 cup

Mayo has a reputation for being boring or, worse, gross. But maybe that's because naysayers haven't tried the homemade stuff yet. Homemade mayonnaise is different from store-bought—it's velvety smooth, more like thickened dressing, and much zippier in flavor.

1 large **pasteurized egg**, at room temperature

1 tablespoon **fresh lemon juice**

1 teaspoon **Dijon mustard**, homemade (see page 28) or store-bought

¼ teaspoon **Himalayan pink salt**

1 cup **avocado oil** or **extra-virgin olive oil**

1. In a medium bowl, whisk together the egg, lemon juice, and mustard. Season with the salt.

2. While whisking continuously, add the avocado oil a teaspoon at a time until you have incorporated about ¼ cup and the mixture has thickened and emulsified. Still whisking continuously, slowly add the remaining oil and whisk until the sauce is thick and silky.

3. Store in an airtight container in the fridge for up to 1 week.

VEGAN AIOLI

Makes 1 cup

We're California girls, and although it's cliché, we definitely try to squeeze avocado into meals wherever and whenever we can. There's a time and place for aioli in every cook's repertoire, and here's Sweet Laurel's version. This vegan aioli, made without eggs, perfectly pairs with a myriad of different foods.

2 ripe medium **avocados**, halved and pitted

1 teaspoon **fresh lemon juice**

2 **garlic cloves**, minced

1 tablespoon **Dijon mustard**, homemade (see page 28) or store-bought

1 teaspoon **Himalayan pink salt**

½ teaspoon **freshly ground black pepper**

¼ cup **olive oil**, plus more for storing

1. Scoop the avocado flesh into a high-speed blender. Add the lemon juice, garlic, mustard, salt, and pepper and blend on medium speed. With the blender running, slowly drizzle in the olive oil until emulsified.

2. Transfer the aioli to a jar and completely cover the surface with a thin layer of oil. Seal the jar and store in the fridge for up to 1 week.

THE BASICS

The building blocks, the foundation, the essential recipes—this is where it all begins. The oven is preheated, your measuring cups are out—it's time to do this. Whether you've been baking for years or this is your first time holding a spatula, we've got you. Grain-free baking breaks many of the conventional baking rules, which is sometimes great—because many times, that means the recipes are a lot simpler. But sometimes that rule-breaking can be unintuitive and confusing. There are tricks and lessons to learn along the way, and we're excited to share some of our favorite recipes with you.

ROUGH PUFF PASTRY

Makes one 15 × 8-inch sheet of pastry dough

Making your own puff pastry is kind of like making your own broth. It's a lot of effort, but it can be incredibly rewarding. Rough puff is a little more simplified and approachable than traditional puff pastry. Instead of folding dough around a slab of butter, then rolling and folding repeatedly to create layers, the butter—or, in our case, ghee—is cut right into the dough. The biggest challenge here will be temperature: if the dough starts to get warm, the fat will melt. If this happens, you won't get a lovely, flaky rise, so be sure to chill the dough for a bit if you feel it getting too soft. (Also, be sure to chill the bowl!) We also recommend making a few sheets of pastry at once and keeping the extras in the freezer. It's always good to have on hand in case of chicken potpie–related emergencies (you know what we're talking about).

1 cup **cassava flour**

¼ cup **arrowroot powder, plus more for dusting**

¼ teaspoon **Himalayan pink salt**

4 ounces (½ cup) plus 5 tablespoons **unsalted ghee, frozen (see Notes)**

10 to 12 tablespoons **ice water**

Notes

The best way to freeze ghee is to place a spoonful from the jar onto piece of parchment paper and place in the freezer until solid.

Chill a large metal bowl in the fridge or freezer ahead of time.

1. In a chilled large metal or glass bowl, sift together the cassava flour, arrowroot, and salt. Using the coarse holes of a box grater, coarsely grate the frozen ghee into the flour, then toss to coat. Drizzle 5 tablespoons of the ice water evenly over the flour mixture and gently stir with a fork until incorporated. Test the mixture by gently squeezing a small handful. It should hold together without crumbling. If it doesn't, add up to an additional tablespoon of water, stir until just incorporated, then test again.

2. Turn out the dough onto a clean surface and form it into a 5-inch square, then wrap it in plastic wrap and refrigerate until firm, about 30 minutes.

3. Place a large piece of parchment paper on a flat surface and sprinkle it with arrowroot. Unwrap the dough, then place the dough on the parchment and place another piece of parchment on top. Roll out the dough to a 15 × 8-inch rectangle. With one long side facing you, fold the short sides of the rectangle in as if you're folding a letter. Don't worry if it splits on the edges—use your fingers to patch up any rips.

4. Wrap the dough in plastic wrap and refrigerate until firm, about 30 minutes. Repeat the entire sequence two more times, then wrap the dough in plastic wrap and refrigerate for at least 1 hour more before using, up to 5 days, or store in the freezer for up to 3 months.

SAVORY TART DOUGH

Makes one 10-inch crust

A good tart crust is a workhorse. It can be used for sweet and savory dishes alike, and can easily move past the world of the fluted tart pan. We love this recipe for galettes and hand pies, or wherever else your imagination takes you. To make it sweeter, simply add a few tablespoons of maple syrup to the batter, or to make it more interesting, add your favorite spices or dried herbs.

1¼ cups **almond flour**

1 cup **arrowroot powder**, plus more for dusting

½ cup **cassava flour**

½ teaspoon **Himalayan pink salt**

½ cup **unsalted ghee** or melted **coconut oil**

2 tablespoons **hot water** (110° to 120°F)

1 large **egg**

1. In a large bowl, sift together the almond flour, arrowroot, cassava flour, and salt until combined.

2. In a food processor, combine the flour mixture, melted ghee, and hot water and process until fully incorporated. Add the egg and pulse just until a dough begins to form. The dough should be moist to the touch but not sticky or wet.

3. Place a large piece of parchment paper on a flat surface and sprinkle it with arrowroot. Turn out the dough onto the parchment. Pat the dough into a ball, then flatten the ball into a ½-inch-thick disk. Wrap the dough in plastic wrap and refrigerate for at least 30 minutes, up to 5 days before using, or store in the freezer for up to 3 months. Thaw frozen dough in the fridge overnight before using in any tart recipe.

NO-BREAD BREAD CRUMBS

Makes 2 cups

When you're following a completely grain-free diet, the little things most people take for granted in recipes, like bread crumbs, become the most frustrating. If you're not a regular baker or don't have gluten-free bread lying around, replacing that one ingredient becomes a much larger task. This is our favorite (and delicious) shortcut, so you don't have to bake a loaf every time you need a garnish. Consider this recipe a blank canvas—feel free to add your favorite herbs and spices to make these bread crumbs your own.

2 cups **almond flour**

1 tablespoon **arrowroot powder**

¼ cup melted **coconut oil**

Pinch of **Himalayan pink salt**

In a medium bowl, combine the almond flour, arrowroot, melted coconut oil, and salt. Gently press the dough together with your fingers until crumbs form. If the mixture feels too dry, add 1 to 2 tablespoons water. Store the bread crumbs in an airtight container in the fridge for up to 10 days.

PIZZA DOUGH

Makes one 10-inch crust

We have a very real and serious personal vendetta against bad gluten-free pizza dough. We've been burned (no pun intended) way too many times to trust it. Pizza is meant to be shared and enjoyed, so having a crust that works is essential for us. We refer back to this recipe in several other recipes throughout this book—we like to keep some dough in our freezer so it's always there when we need it. If you like, once you've assembled the dough, you can let it sit on the counter and ferment a bit longer (up to 2 hours) for a slightly more "sour" pizza crust.

1½ cups **almond flour**

1 cup **arrowroot powder**, plus more for dusting

½ teaspoon **Himalayan pink salt**

¼ cup **coconut yogurt**, homemade (see page 26) or store-bought

½ cup **unsweetened almond milk**

1. In a medium bowl, combine the almond flour, arrowroot, and salt. Slowly stir in the coconut yogurt and almond milk and mix with a wooden spoon until a soft dough forms, about 1 minute.

2. Place a large piece of parchment paper on a flat surface and sprinkle it with arrowroot. Turn out the dough onto the parchment and roll it out to a 10-inch round. Use as directed in our pizza recipes (see pages 227 to 231), or wrap tightly in plastic wrap and store in the freezer for up to 3 months. Thaw frozen dough overnight in the fridge before using.

BASIC PASTA DOUGH

Makes 1 pound pasta dough

We believe everyone is either a pizza person or a pasta person. You can always enjoy both, but only one truly has your heart. There is a lot of internal debate on the subject. We won't say who's who, but one of us is a pizza person and the other is a die-hard pasta nut. Pasta has the ability to transform into long sheets for a hearty lasagna (see page 260), or a cozy accent in soup (see page 162), or a decadent mac and cheese—what's not to love?

1 cup blanched almond flour

1 cup tapioca flour

¾ cup arrowroot powder, plus more for dusting

2 teaspoons Himalayan pink salt

2 large eggs

3 large egg yolks

2 tablespoons extra-virgin olive oil

1. In the bowl of a stand mixer fitted with the dough hook, combine the almond flour, tapioca flour, arrowroot, and salt and beat on medium speed until fully incorporated.

2. In a small bowl, whisk together the eggs, egg yolks, and olive oil. With the mixer running on low, slowly add the egg mixture and beat until a smooth ball of dough forms, about 12 minutes. If needed, add water 1 tablespoon at a time (up to 4 tablespoons) to help the dough come together. It should be damp but not sticky or wet.

3. Divide the dough into 4 equal portions and lightly wrap 3 of them in plastic wrap to keep them from drying out while you roll out the dough. Run the dough through a pasta maker or stand mixer fitted with the pasta attachment to create sheets of pasta about ⅛ inch thick. (You are not developing any gluten, so there's no need to fold and reroll or press the dough as you would if you were making traditional wheat flour–based pasta.) Alternatively, dust a flat surface and rolling pin with arrowroot powder and roll out the dough as thinly as possible, about ⅛ inch thick.

4. Lay the sheets of pasta on a flat surface. Using a sharp knife, cut the pasta into your desired shapes. Lightly dust the pasta with arrowroot powder to prevent sticking. Use immediately, or store in an airtight container in the fridge for up to 5 days or in the freezer for up to 3 months. Thaw frozen dough overnight in the fridge before using.

PITAS

Makes 8 pitas

Laurel grew up in a huge Greek family, with cousins crowded around meze platters loaded with cucumbers, hummus, olives, and tzatziki sauce (our favorite—see page 147), all served with a mountain of pita. Creating a grain-free pita with that coveted, characteristic pocket was our goal, and we're happy to say we accomplished it. These make the perfect vessel for crunchy falafel (see page 194).

1 heaping tablespoon **active dry yeast**

1 tablespoon **pure maple syrup**

¾ cup **warm water (100° to 110°F)**

1 cup **almond flour**

2½ cups **arrowroot powder**

1 teaspoon **ground chia seeds**

½ teaspoon **Himalayan pink salt**

1 large **egg white**

2 tablespoons **avocado oil**, plus more for cooking

1. In a small bowl, combine the yeast, maple syrup, and ½ cup of the warm water. Let sit in a warm area—in direct sunlight, for instance (about 80°F is ideal)—until foaming and bubbling, 5 to 10 minutes.

2. In a medium bowl, combine the almond flour, arrowroot, chia, salt, egg white, avocado oil, and the remaining ¼ cup warm water. Mix well, then add the yeast mixture. Cover with a damp kitchen towel and let sit at room temperature for 35 minutes to 1 hour, until risen slightly.

3. Lightly oil a medium skillet and heat over medium heat. When the oil is shimmering, add ¼ cup of the batter and, using a rubber spatula, smooth it out into a circle about 4 inches in diameter and ¼ inch thick. Cook until lightly browned on both sides, 4 to 5 minutes per side. Remove the pita from the skillet and carefully cut a slit along the edge to create a pocket. Continue cutting around the edge until half of the pita has been opened. Set aside on a plate lined with a tea towel to keep the pita warm. Repeat with the remaining batter, adding more oil to the skillet after cooking each pita.

4. Serve warm, or let cool, then stack the pitas and wrap in plastic wrap. Store in the fridge for up to 1 week or in the freezer for up to 3 months. Reheat the pitas in the oven or microwave before serving, thawing completely first if using frozen ones.

RAINBOW TORTILLAS

Makes four 5-inch tortillas

As LA girls with a love of Mexican cuisine, we needed our tortillas to not only look the part but taste and feel the same, too. The flax egg here mimics the slight grit of masa, and the combination of arrowroot and cassava creates a yielding texture. And these tortillas can go beyond tacos. They're perfect for wrapping fresh vegetables with delicious sauces, making quesadillas, or grilling to serve on a beautiful meze platter. Inspired by the colors and variety of tortillas you'll find across Mexico, we made ours rainbow-colored with natural flavors, which you can take or leave as you like.

¼ cup plus 2 tablespoons **arrowroot powder**

¼ cup plus 2 tablespoons **cassava flour**

¼ teaspoon **Himalayan pink salt**

1 **flax egg** (see page 27)

3 tablespoons **avocado oil**

OPTIONAL COLORINGS

1 tablespoon **matcha powder** (for green)

1 teaspoon **ground turmeric** (for yellow)

1 tablespoon **beet juice** (for pink)

1 tablespoon **butterfly pea flower tea**, steeped (for blue)

1. In a medium bowl, combine the arrowroot, cassava flour, and salt. (If you'd like to color the tortillas green, add the matcha here; for yellow tortillas, add the turmeric.) Add the flax egg, oil, and ⅓ cup water and stir to combine. (If you'd like to color the tortillas pink, add the beet juice here; for blue, add the butterfly pea flower tea.)

2. Form the dough into four 2-inch balls. Flatten the balls in a tortilla press, or place the dough between two pieces of parchment paper and roll them into rounds about 5 inches in diameter and ⅛ inch thick.

3. Place a medium skillet over medium-high heat. One at a time, add the tortillas and cook for about 1 minute on each side, until deep golden brown spots start to form. To keep warm, place the hot tortillas inside a folded clean kitchen towel until ready to serve.

4. To store the tortillas, let them cool, then stack them, placing a piece of parchment between each tortilla, and wrap them in plastic wrap. Store in the fridge for up to 2 weeks or in the freezer for up to 3 months. Warm the tortillas in a skillet or microwave for 10 seconds before serving.

What's your spirit cheese? The cheese that sums you up as a person? Claire asks this question at dinner parties and then makes sure that her cheese boards are populated with some delicious representation of all her friends. For her husband, it's burrata; for her brother, it's washed-rind cheese that makes your eyes water; and for the longest time, Laurel would have to pass—on the game and on the cheese board. But over the years, the world of nut-based cheeses has bloomed (cheese mold pun very much intended). When we think about savory recipes, we are inspired by all the melty, gooey dishes Laurel has been able to return to: macaroni and cheese (see page 130), pizza bianca (see page 231), and lasagna (see page 260), just to name a few. Our cheeses are simple to make—they're all essentially nut milk or coconut milk and an acid—and such delicious ways to top our recipes.

DAIRY-FREE CHEESE

CHEESE SAUCE

Makes 1½ cups

2 cups **cashews**, soaked overnight and drained

2½ tablespoons **nutritional yeast**

½ teaspoon **Himalayan pink salt**

½ teaspoon **smoked paprika**

½ teaspoon **onion powder**

½ teaspoon **garlic powder**

½ teaspoon **freshly ground white pepper**

¼ teaspoon **grated nutmeg**

1 teaspoon **ground turmeric** (optional, for color)

¼ cup **unsalted ghee** or **extra-virgin olive oil**

3 tablespoons **arrowroot powder**

1 tablespoon **coconut butter**

1. In a high-speed blender or food processor, combine the soaked cashews, 4 cups water, the nutritional yeast, salt, paprika, onion powder, garlic powder, white pepper, nutmeg, and turmeric (if using) and blend on high until fully combined, about 2 minutes.

2. In a medium saucepan, melt the ghee over medium heat. Whisk in the arrowroot and coconut butter, and cook, whisking continuously, until the mixture bubbles and thickens, about 2 minutes, being careful not to let it brown. Slowly whisk in the cashew mixture and bring to a simmer. The cashew sauce should be velvety and thick. If it gets too thick or gummy, whisk in a little more water.

3. Use immediately, or let cool and store in an airtight container in the fridge for up to 1 week.

CLASSIC VEGAN CREAM CHEESE

Makes 2 cups

2 cups **cashews, macadamia nuts,** or **pine nuts,** soaked overnight and drained

1 tablespoon **nutritional yeast**

2 teaspoons **cider vinegar**

½ teaspoon **Himalayan pink salt**

1. In a high-speed blender, combine the soaked nuts, 1 cup water, the nutritional yeast, vinegar, and salt and blend until creamy, about 3 minutes.

2. Line a colander with cheesecloth and set it over a medium bowl. Pour the nut mixture into the cheesecloth and squeeze it into the shape of a log, twisting the cheesecloth tight at the left and right ends so it looks like a wrapped candy. Place the log in a warm, draft-free area to ferment for 8 to 12 hours, twisting the cheesecloth and squeezing out excess liquid every 2 hours.

3. Remove the cheesecloth and wrap the log of cream cheese in parchment paper. Refrigerate until ready to serve. We like to smooth the cream cheese into a small dish for easy spreading. It will keep in the fridge for up to 5 days.

DAIRY-FREE FETA

¾ cup **raw cashews**, soaked for at least 3 hours or up to overnight and drained

6 tablespoons **coconut oil**

¼ cup **fresh lemon juice**

1 tablespoon **tahini**

1 teaspoon **nutritional yeast**

¼ teaspoon **Himalayan pink salt**

1. In a food processor, combine the soaked cashews, oil, lemon juice, tahini, nutritional yeast, and salt and pulse until creamy. Add up to 2 tablespoons water as needed to smooth the mixture.

2. Line a colander with cheesecloth and set it over a medium bowl. Pour the mixture into the cheesecloth and use the cheesecloth to roll the mixture into a 6-inch-long log. Let the cheesecloth set at room temperature for 12 hours, or until drained and firm.

3. Preheat the oven to 200°F.

4. Place the log of cheese in a small baking dish, twisting the cheesecloth tight at the left and right sides so it looks like a wrapped candy. Bake the cheese, turning it occasionally, until firm and dry, about 35 minutes. Remove from the oven and let cool completely.

5. Remove the cheesecloth and crumble the cheese. Store in an airtight container in the fridge for up to 5 days.

DAIRY-FREE PARMESAN

½ cup **coconut butter**

1 tablespoon **fresh lemon juice**

¼ cup **nutritional yeast**

1 **probiotic capsule**

½ teaspoon **Himalayan pink salt**

1 teaspoon **onion powder**

1 teaspoon **garlic powder**

½ teaspoon **freshly ground white pepper**

½ cup **avocado oil**

1. In a small saucepan, heat the coconut butter over low heat for about 5 minutes, being careful not to let it brown.

2. In a high-speed blender, combine the melted coconut butter, lemon juice, nutritional yeast, the contents of the probiotic capsule, salt, onion powder, garlic powder, white pepper, and oil and blend until fully combined, about 30 seconds. Pour into a glass jar and seal it. Let sit at room temperature for about 5 hours, until the mixture smells tart like yogurt.

3. Lay a large piece of parchment paper on a clean surface. Pour the mixture onto the parchment and roll it into a 2-inch-thick log. Refrigerate the log for 5 hours, or until the mixture has hardened.

4. To serve, gently unroll the parchment and shave or cut off pieces of the cheese. Store the cheese in an airtight container in the fridge for up to 2 weeks.

DAIRY-FREE MOZZARELLA

Makes 1 cup

⅓ cup cassava flour

1 cup full-fat canned coconut milk

2 tablespoons coconut oil

2 teaspoons cider vinegar

1 teaspoon Himalayan pink salt

1. In a medium bowl, stir together ¾ cup water and the cassava flour until smooth.

2. In a medium saucepan, combine the coconut milk, coconut oil, vinegar, and salt and cook over low heat, stirring, until the mixture is evenly combined and slightly warm, about 4 minutes.

3. Slowly stir the flour mixture into the coconut milk mixture and cook, stirring continuously, until thick and pulling away from the edges of the pan, about 7 minutes. Pour the mixture into a glass container, cover, and refrigerate for at least 3 hours, until it has solidified.

4. Store in an airtight container in the fridge for up to 5 days.

DAIRY-FREE CHEDDAR CHEESE

Makes 1½ cups

⅓ cup cassava flour

1 cup coconut milk

2 tablespoons coconut oil or unsalted ghee

1½ teaspoons cider vinegar

1 teaspoon nutritional yeast

1 teaspoon Himalayan pink salt

½ teaspoon ground turmeric

½ teaspoon paprika

½ teaspoon garlic powder

1. In a medium bowl, stir together ¾ cup water and the cassava flour until smooth.

2. In a medium saucepan, combine the coconut milk, coconut oil, vinegar, nutritional yeast, salt, turmeric, paprika, and garlic powder and cook over medium heat, stirring slowly, until the mixture is evenly combined and slightly warm, about 4 minutes.

3. Slowly add the flour mixture to the coconut milk mixture and cook, stirring continuously, until very thick and pulling away from the edges of the pan, about 10 minutes. Pour into a glass container, cover, and refrigerate for 3 to 4 hours, until solidified.

4. Serve the cheese as you would serve cheddar— slice and melt as desired. Store in an airtight container in the fridge for up to 5 days.

part two

The recipes in the chapter will help you get familiar with grain-free baking. All these recipes should be served alongside dishes for dipping and spreading or used as the base for something special. Consider these your new go-to recipes for their delicious flavors and simple processes. Here's to a breadbasket filled with endless, savory possibilities.

LOAVES, ROLLS, *and* QUICK BREADS

A SIMPLIFIED APPROACH
TO GRAIN-FREE BAKING

If you're familiar with baking conventional yeasted breads, you should know there are a few "rules" that will go straight out the window when you're baking by the Sweet Laurel method. It might seem counterintuitive at first, but it's actually a simplified approach that can help even the newest baker feel confident in the kitchen.

BROKEN RULE 1:

"Bread dough should be kneaded."

Dough made with wheat flour (or any flour that contains gluten) must be kneaded to develop gluten, which creates structure—otherwise, you'd end up with a dense pancake instead of a buoyant, light loaf. But grain-free baking recipes do not contain any gluten, so there is no need to knead. In fact, kneading gluten-free dough just makes a mess. Instead, our bread dough is mixed in a bowl, either with your hands or a spatula, and often has the consistency of a thick batter.

BROKEN RULE 2:

"Bread dough should not be wet."

The reason you can throw conventional pizza dough into the air and stretch it easily is, again, because of the gluten within it. Conventional dough should be pliable and tacky to the touch—never wet—and ready to stretch and form. But with grain-free baking, if the dough is dry enough to throw in the air or knead together, you'll have a brick instead of a loaf when it's done baking. In order to get bubbly, aerated bread, your grain-free dough needs quite a bit of liquid. During baking, the liquid creates steam, which, in turn, creates air bubbles in the dough—that's how grain-free bread gets a light texture. Most of our doughs are meant to be poured into a loaf pan or rolled between two sheets of parchment paper, which means they're too wet to handle like conventional dough. Here, wet dough is a good thing!

BROKEN RULE 3:

"Bake at high heat for a quick rise and a crunchy crust."

If you were baking a conventional sourdough loaf, preheating your oven almost to its maximum temperature is necessary. The super-high heat creates steam and lift in the dough, and the high heat creates that deeply caramelized crust. With grain-free baking, however, such high heat will create lift and a caramelized crust—but leave a soggy interior. You'll notice that most of our recipes call for lower baking temperatures to encourage a perfectly fluffy interior and a slowly caramelized crust.

BRIOCHE

Claire's first experience with brioche was at a hotel breakfast buffet in Japan. A perfect creamy yellow hue, a fine, almost cakelike crumb, it was practically begging to be toasted. This particular toaster held only one slice at a time; it sealed in the bread's moisture, and blasted it at 500°F. Out came a delicate, golden brown pillow of perfection. Fluffy on the inside, perfectly crisp on the outside—a piece of toasted brioche is truly a simple, good thing. This experience was the inspiration for our brioche recipe—simple and good. We love it toasted with jam, but it makes incredible sandwich bread and is fantastic for French toast, too.

Coconut oil or ghee, for greasing

2 heaping tablespoons active dry yeast

1 cup warm water (100° to 110°F)

2 cups arrowroot powder

2 cups almond flour

4 teaspoons baking powder, homemade (see page 28) or store-bought

1 teaspoon Himalayan pink salt

2 tablespoons pure maple syrup

¼ cup cider vinegar

6 large eggs, separated, plus 1 large egg

1. Preheat the oven to 325°F. Line an 8 × 4-inch loaf pan with parchment paper, letting the paper hang over the sides for easy removal, and lightly grease the parchment with coconut oil.

2. In a small bowl, combine the yeast and warm water. Let sit in a warm area—in direct sunlight, for instance (about 80°F is ideal)—until foaming and bubbling, 5 to 10 minutes.

3. In a medium bowl, combine the arrowroot, almond flour, baking powder, and salt. Stir in the yeast mixture, maple syrup, vinegar, and egg yolks. It will have the texture of a thick batter. Let sit for about 1 hour, until bubbles form on the surface of the dough.

4. In a small bowl, whisk the egg for the egg wash with 1 teaspoon water. Set aside.

5. In a separate medium bowl, using a handheld mixer, beat the egg whites on high until fluffy, about 2 minutes. Gently fold the egg whites into the dough. Transfer the dough to the prepared loaf pan. Bake for 50 to 55 minutes, until golden brown on top and nicely puffed. A toothpick inserted into the center should come out clean. Let cool in the pan completely, about an hour, before slicing and serving.

6. Wrap the bread in plastic wrap and store on the counter for 3 to 4 days or in the freezer for up to 3 months.

RUSTIC LOAF

A truly rustic loaf of bread, created in the Old World European fashion, has always felt beyond the reach of grain- and gluten-free bakers—and for a good reason. In order for that delicious, robust flavor to come through, yeast partners with gluten to develop the structure needed for a chewy interior and perfectly crisp crust. To replicate this effect without gluten, we used sweet potatoes and flax meal for hearty texture and flavor. These tricks get us a delicious alternative—chewy, crisp, and ready to dip in a bowl of olive oil with a sprinkling of salt.

1 cup chopped peeled **sweet potato** (see Note)

¼ cup **avocado oil**, plus more for greasing

4 **large eggs**

1 tablespoon **cider vinegar**

⅔ cup **coconut flour**

2 tablespoons **psyllium husk**

2 tablespoons **flax meal**

1 teaspoon **baking soda**

½ teaspoon **Himalayan pink salt**

Note

We prefer to use white sweet potatoes for their color in this recipe, but any kind will work.

1. Preheat the oven to 400°F. Line an 8 × 4-inch loaf pan with parchment paper, letting the paper hang over the sides for easy removal.

2. In a blender or food processor, combine the sweet potato, avocado oil, eggs, vinegar, and ⅓ cup water and blend until completely smooth, 2 to 3 minutes.

3. In medium bowl, combine the coconut flour, psyllium husk, flax meal, baking soda, and salt. Add the sweet potato mixture and mix with a spatula until a soft dough forms.

4. Line a work surface with parchment. Turn out the dough onto the parchment and form it into a ball, then shape the ball into a small loaf, slightly smaller than the prepared pan. Place the loaf in the pan and bake for about 40 minutes, until golden brown on top and nicely puffed. Let cool in the pan for 15 minutes, then take out the bread and let cool completely on a wire rack before slicing and serving.

5. Wrap the bread in plastic wrap and store on the counter for 3 to 4 days or in the freezer for up to 3 months.

PERFECT SANDWICH BREAD

Makes one 8 × 4-inch loaf

Claire has "sandwich queen" in her blood. Her gran would bake her own bread, grow her own tomatoes, and probably milk her own cows for butter to make the ultimate tomato sandwich: delicately toasted bread, a swish of butter, slabs of tomatoes, a touch of salt, finished with a mountain of black pepper. This simple sandwich all starts with the bread. Our sandwich bread is meant to be versatile and simple, hearty enough for a BLT (see page 197) but delicate enough to serve as toast at brunch, smothered with fresh jam or marmalade . . . or tomatoes, butter, and a little too much black pepper.

2 tablespoons **active dry yeast**

1 cup **warm water** (100° to 110°F)

2 tablespoons **pure maple syrup**

2 cups **almond flour**

1 cup **arrowroot powder**

1 cup **cassava flour**

4 teaspoons **baking powder**, homemade (see page 28) or store-bought

1 teaspoon **Himalayan pink salt**

¼ cup **cider vinegar**

6 **large eggs**, separated

2 **flax eggs** (see page 27; these add texture to the loaf)

1. Line an 8 × 4-inch loaf pan with parchment paper, letting the paper hang over the sides for easy removal.

2. In a small bowl, combine the yeast, warm water, and maple syrup. Let sit in a warm area—in direct sunlight, for instance (about 80°F is ideal)—until foaming and bubbling, 5 to 10 minutes.

3. In a medium bowl, combine the almond flour, arrowroot, cassava flour, baking powder, and salt. Stir in the yeast mixture, vinegar, egg yolks, and flax eggs until fully incorporated. Cover the bowl with a damp kitchen towel. Let the mixture sit in a warm area for about 1 hour, until slightly puffed.

4. Preheat the oven to 325°F.

5. In a medium bowl, using a handheld mixer, beat the egg whites on high until fluffy, about 2 minutes. Fold the egg whites into the dough and pour the dough into the prepared pan. Bake for 60 to 75 minutes, until a toothpick inserted into the center comes out clean. Let cool in the pan completely, about 1 hour, before slicing and serving.

6. Wrap the bread in plastic wrap and store on the counter for 3 to 4 days or in the freezer for up to 3 months.

CARAWAY "RYE" BREAD

We both grew up about ten blocks from (in our opinion) the best twenty-four-hour deli in LA—Izzy's, where a single pastrami on rye sandwich was enough for three meals. Laurel grew up calling this rye bread "Daddy's Bread," because he would have a piece of it spread with butter every night at dinner. Rye bread is nostalgic for us, not only because of these memories but also because that's just what hearty brown bread does: it sends us back to an earlier time, when loaves weren't perfectly white and ready to be cut to crustless. But our version of course doesn't use rye, which is a grain; it does, however, get at that classic rye earthiness from the traditional caraway seeds and the flax, which lends it a rustic hue. This bread is delicious with a swipe of our cream cheese (see page 44) and some smoked salmon on top.

Coconut oil, for greasing

1¼ cups **almond flour**

1 cup **flax meal**

¼ cup **caraway seeds**

1 teaspoon **baking soda**

½ teaspoon **Himalayan pink salt**

1 cup **cashew butter**

4 large **eggs**

4 large **egg whites**

2 tablespoons **water**

2 tablespoons **cider vinegar**

1. Preheat the oven to 350°F. Line an 8 × 4-inch loaf pan with parchment paper, letting the paper hang over the sides for easy removal, and lightly grease the parchment with coconut oil.

2. In a medium bowl, combine the almond flour, flax meal, caraway seeds, baking soda, and salt.

3. In the bowl of a stand mixer fitted with the paddle attachment, combine the cashew butter, eggs, and egg whites and beat on medium until smooth. With the mixer running, slowly pour in 2 tablespoons water, then add the dry ingredients and the vinegar and beat until smooth.

4. Pour the batter into the prepared pan and bake for 60 to 75 minutes, until a toothpick inserted into the center comes out clean. Let cool in the pan for 15 minutes, then take out the bread and let cool completely on a wire rack before slicing and serving.

5. Wrap the bread in plastic wrap and store on the counter for 3 to 4 days or in the freezer for up to 3 months.

GREEN OLIVE BREAD

Makes one 8-inch round loaf

In a bakery window of the Roman bakery Antico Forno Roscioli, cross sections of olive bread create a kaleidoscope of texture. When we saw it on our travels through Italy, we knew we needed to create something like it back home. Cutting into the loaf reveals gorgeous, deep green polka dots of olives, and the scent is warm and inviting. We love serving this loaf lightly toasted, with something special to dip it in (like our Sun-Dried Tomato Dip on page 148, for instance). If you prefer the robust flavor of Greek olives or the savory saltiness of cured olives, you can use any of those here in place of the green olives—just make sure they're pitted!

4½ teaspoons **active dry yeast**

1 tablespoon **honey**

⅔ cup **warm water** (100° to 110°F)

2½ cups **almond flour**

1¼ cups **arrowroot powder**

¼ cup **tapioca starch**

1 teaspoon **Himalayan pink salt**

1 tablespoon **extra-virgin olive oil**, plus more as needed

3 large **egg whites**

1 teaspoon **cider vinegar**

1½ cups **pitted green olives** (Castelvetrano olives are our favorite)

1. In a small bowl, combine the yeast, honey, and warm water. Let sit in a warm area—in direct sunlight, for instance (about 80°F is ideal)—until foaming and bubbling, 5 to 10 minutes.

2. In the bowl of a stand mixer fitted with the paddle attachment, combine the almond flour, arrowroot, tapioca starch, salt, and yeast mixture and beat on medium speed until combined. Add the olive oil and egg whites and beat until combined. Add the vinegar, increase the speed to high, and beat for 2 minutes more, or until a thick batter forms. Using a spatula, fold in the olives.

3. Place the dough in a lightly oiled bowl and cover with a damp kitchen towel and let the dough rise for 1 to 2 hours, until it has expanded by about one-third.

4. Meanwhile, preheat the oven to 375°F. Line an 8-inch round or 10-inch oval baking dish with parchment paper and lightly grease the parchment with olive oil.

5. Transfer the dough to the prepared baking dish and bake for 40 to 45 minutes, until the bread is golden brown. Remove the bread from the oven and set the baking dish on a wire rack to cool for 15 minutes before serving.

6. Serve the bread slightly warm, with a dish of olive oil for dipping. Wrapped in plastic wrap, it will keep at room temperature for 3 to 4 days.

SWEET AND SAVORY HONEY "CORN BREAD"

Makes one 9-inch round loaf (8 to 10 servings)

A cup of chili, a plate of ribs—yet life seems incomplete without a wedge of corn bread on the side. But corn can be inflammatory for many people, including Laurel, and those who can't handle processed grains often can't handle corn. Corn bread without the corn sounds impossible, but this fluffy, sweet bread has tricked both of our husbands more than once. The keys are the subtle sweetness from the honey and the bite from the natural almond flour and flax meal. Turmeric creates the golden hue of traditional corn bread. Try folding in some sliced scallions, jalapeños, and cheddar cheese (see page 47 for our dairy-free cheddar) if you want to feel extra fancy.

¼ cup **avocado oil**, plus more for greasing

1½ cups **almond flour**

¼ cup **coconut flour**

¼ cup **flax meal**

1 tablespoon **baking powder**, homemade (see page 28) or store-bought

½ teaspoon **Himalayan pink salt**

½ teaspoon **ground turmeric**

4 **large eggs** or **flax eggs** (see page 27), at room temperature

¼ cup **honey** or **pure maple syrup**

1 cup **almond milk**, homemade (see page 26) or store-bought

1 teaspoon **cider vinegar**

Whipped ghee and/or **honey**, for serving

1. Preheat the oven to 350°F. Grease a 9-inch cast-iron skillet with avocado oil.

2. In a large bowl, whisk together the almond flour, coconut flour, flax meal, baking powder, salt, and turmeric.

3. In a medium bowl, whisk together the eggs, honey, almond milk, oil, and vinegar until well incorporated. Add the wet ingredients to the dry ingredients and stir until a batter forms.

4. Pour the batter into the prepared pan and bake for 40 minutes, or until lightly golden brown and a toothpick inserted into the center comes out clean. Cut into 2-inch squares and enjoy warm, with some whipped ghee and/or honey alongside. Leftovers can be refrigerated in an air-tight container for up to 5 days.

ROSEMARY ROASTED GARLIC FOCACCIA

If we had our own "small pleasures" sequence like in the film *Amélie*, sticking our fingers into soft, warm bread dough would be ours. It's a strange, tactile satisfaction. Baking is meant to be a hands-on experience, but creating grain-free breads, which are usually made with more of a batter than a dough, can sometimes feel a little disconnected from the physical act of baking. Not so with this recipe, which encourages hands-on handling, as with traditional focaccia. So get ready to get your hands dirty, because this recipe is worth it.

1 head **garlic**

1 tablespoon **olive oil**

FOR THE DOUGH

2 teaspoons **active dry yeast**

2 teaspoons **pure maple syrup or honey**

¼ cup **warm water** (100° to 110°F)

2¼ cups **almond flour**

1½ cups **arrowroot powder**

1½ teaspoons **baking powder**, homemade (see page 28) or store-bought

½ teaspoon **Himalayan pink salt**

1 large **egg**, at room temperature

3 large **egg whites**, at room temperature

Extra-virgin olive oil

2 teaspoons **cider vinegar**

2 teaspoons coarsely chopped **fresh rosemary**, plus more for garnish

Flaky sea salt

1. Preheat the oven to 400°F.

2. Chop off the top half of the garlic head to reveal the cloves. Peel off any excess papery skin from the head, being sure to keep the head intact. Place the garlic on a small piece of aluminum foil. Drizzle with the olive oil and wrap the foil around the garlic to enclose it completely. Roast for 30 to 40 minutes, until the cloves are golden brown and soft. Remove the garlic from the foil and let cool slightly. Squeeze the cloves into a small bowl, discarding the papery skins, and set aside to cool.

3. Make the dough. In a large bowl, combine the yeast, maple syrup, and warm water. Cover with a damp kitchen towel and let sit in a warm area—in direct sunlight, for instance (about 80°F is ideal)—until foaming and bubbling, 5 to 10 minutes.

4. In a medium bowl, whisk together the almond flour, arrowroot, baking powder, and Himalayan pink salt until fully combined.

5. Add the egg, egg whites, roasted garlic cloves, 1 tablespoon extra-virgin olive oil, and vinegar to the bowl with the yeast mixture. Using a whisk or a handheld mixer on low, mix for 2 to 3 minutes, until light and frothy. Add the flour mixture and the rosemary in two batches and mix until a soft dough forms. Cover with a damp kitchen towel and let the dough rise for 1 to 2 hours, until it has expanded by about 30 percent.

6. Line a 10-inch skillet or baking dish with parchment paper and grease the skillet and parchment with extra-virgin olive oil.

7. Transfer the dough to the prepared skillet. Dip a spatula or your fingers in water and spread the dough to an even thickness in the skillet.

With wet fingers, make indentations in the dough. It's fine if they're a bit irregular—it makes the focaccia look more rustic. Sprinkle the dough with rosemary and flaky salt, then drizzle generously with extra-virgin olive oil. Cover with a clean kitchen towel and place in a warm place for 40 to 50 minutes, until noticeably risen and a bit puffy.

8. Preheat the oven to 375°F.

9. Bake for 30 to 32 minutes, until the bread is golden brown. Remove the focaccia from the skillet, set on a rack, and let cool for 15 minutes before serving.

10. Serve this bread slightly warm, with a dish of extra-virgin olive oil for dipping. Wrapped in plastic wrap, it will keep at room temperature for 3 to 4 days.

GARLIC PULL-APART BREAD

You'll want to bake this pull-apart bread for the smell alone—it's that incredible. It lures people out of their private corners of the house and into the kitchen to see what's for dinner. Have a kid at home who's resigned to playing in their room all day? A partner who tucks away for hours working in a nook? Bake this bread to get them in the kitchen immediately.

FOR THE GARLIC PASTE

⅓ cup plus 2 tablespoons **unsalted ghee** or **extra-virgin olive oil**

2 tablespoons **extra-virgin olive oil**

1 head **garlic**, cloves separated, smashed, and peeled

Large handful of **fresh flat-leaf parsley leaves**, finely chopped

Himalayan pink salt and **freshly ground black pepper**

FOR THE BREAD

2½ tablespoons **unsalted ghee**, melted and cooled, plus more for greasing

3 cups **almond flour**

¾ cup **arrowroot powder**, plus more for dusting

6 tablespoons **golden flax meal**

2¼ teaspoons **baking powder**, homemade (see page 28) or store-bought

1½ teaspoons **Himalayan pink salt**

3 large **eggs**, at room temperature

¼ cup **coconut cream**

1 tablespoon **cider vinegar**

1. Make the garlic paste. In a food processor, combine the ghee, olive oil, garlic, parsley, salt, and pepper and pulse until smooth. Set aside.

2. Preheat the oven to 375°F. Grease an 8 × 4-inch loaf pan with ghee.

3. Make the bread. In a medium bowl, whisk together the almond flour, arrowroot, flax meal, baking powder, and salt.

4. In a large bowl, using a handheld mixer, beat the eggs, coconut cream, 1½ tablespoons melted ghee, and vinegar on medium until combined, 1 to 2 minutes. Add the dry ingredients and mix to combine. The dough will become sticky, so work quickly. Use a wet spatula or a plastic dough scraper to gather the dough into a ball.

5. Turn out the dough onto a sheet of parchment paper lightly dusted with arrowroot, sprinkle the dough with a little arrowroot, and cover with another sheet of parchment. Using a rolling pin, roll out the dough to a ½-inch-thick rectangle. Remove the top piece of parchment and spread the garlic paste evenly over the dough. With a short edge nearest you, roll up the dough, enclosing the garlic paste, creating a log. Slice the dough crosswise into 1-inch-wide pieces, then quarter the slices into 1-inch portions. Roll each portion into a ball with your hands.

6. Place the dough balls into the prepared loaf pan—they should be distinct spheres but touching and layered on top of one another. Bake for 30 to 40 minutes, until deep golden brown, loosely covering the pan with aluminum foil halfway through but being careful not to rest the foil directly on the dough.

7. Remove the loaf from the oven and brush with 1 tablespoon melted ghee. Let cool in the pan for 20 minutes, then invert the loaf onto a serving plate. Serve immediately. Store the bread, wrapped in plastic wrap, at room temperature for 3 to 4 days.

SESAME-STUDDED BURGER BUNS

The burger is in the eye of the beholder. Some people love a thick, Au Cheval–style pub burger, but others, including us, go for the LA-style smash burger: crispy, salty, juicy, and smushed between two soft buns. Whatever your favorite burger, it'll taste good on our burger buns. They are fluffy perfection; we love them classic, studded with sesame seeds. The key to getting even, perfectly puffed burger buns with this recipe is using a 3-ounce ice cream scoop to portion the dough onto your baking dish.

1 heaping tablespoon **active dry yeast**

1 tablespoon **pure maple syrup**

¼ cup **warm water (100° to 110°F)**

2 cups **almond flour**

1 cup **arrowroot powder**

¼ cup **cassava flour**

2 teaspoons **baking powder,** homemade (see page 28) or store-bought

½ teaspoon **Himalayan pink salt**

2 tablespoons **cider vinegar**

4 large **eggs**, separated

¼ cup **sesame seeds**

1. In a small bowl, combine the yeast, maple syrup, and warm water. Let sit in a warm area—in direct sunlight, for instance (about 80°F is ideal)—until foaming and bubbling, 5 to 10 minutes.

2. In a medium bowl, combine the almond flour, arrowroot, cassava flour, baking powder, and salt. Stir in the yeast mixture, vinegar, and egg yolks. Cover the bowl with a clean kitchen towel. Let the dough sit in a warm area for about 1 hour, until slightly puffed.

3. Preheat the oven to 350°F. Line a baking sheet with parchment paper.

4. In a medium bowl, using a handheld mixer, beat the egg whites on high until fluffy, about 2 minutes. Fold the egg whites into the dough. With a ⅓-cup measuring cup or 3-ounce ice cream scoop, scoop the dough onto the prepared baking sheet, spacing the buns about 1½ inches apart, and sprinkle the tops with the sesame seeds. Bake for about 18 minutes, until just golden brown.

5. Transfer the buns to a wire rack and let cool completely, about 20 minutes. We use one bun for the crown and another bun for the heel of the hamburger.

6. Store the buns, wrapped in plastic wrap, on the counter for 3 to 4 days or in the freezer for up to 3 months.

SWEET POTATO ROLLS

You know that moment when you're eating breakfast, and your bacon and maple syrup accidentally touch? Well, that's the exact flavor space these rolls live in. They hover between the sweet and savory—our favorite line to blur. Try glazing them with maple syrup and serving them with berries for a just-sweet-enough breakfast. They're great on their own, too!

4 ounces **sweet potato**, peeled and cut into 1-inch pieces

2 cups **cassava flour**

1 tablespoon **coconut flour**

1½ teaspoons **Himalayan pink salt**

¼ teaspoon **ground cinnamon**

1 cup **avocado oil** or **coconut oil**

2 tablespoons **pure maple syrup**

5 **large eggs**

1. Preheat the oven to 350°F. Line a baking sheet with parchment paper.

2. Put the sweet potato in a small pot and add water to cover. Bring to a boil over high heat, then reduce the heat to maintain a simmer and cook for about 10 minutes, until the sweet potatoes can be easily pierced with a knife. Drain, then transfer the sweet potatoes to a bowl and mash lightly with a potato masher. Set aside and cool to room temperature.

3. In a large bowl, combine the cassava flour, coconut flour, salt, and cinnamon. Stir in the cooked sweet potato, avocado oil, and maple syrup until fully incorporated, then fold in 4 of the eggs. If the mixture is too dry and won't come together fully, add up to 2 tablespoons water.

4. Beat the remaining egg with 1 teaspoon water to make an egg wash. Divide the dough into 12 equal portions and, using your hands, roll each into a ball. Place them on the prepared baking sheet about 1½ inches apart and brush each roll with the egg wash. Bake for 15 to 20 minutes, until just golden brown.

5. Serve immediately. Wrap the pan in plastic wrap and store on the counter for 3 to 4 days or in the freezer for up to 3 months. Reheat in the oven.

CLASSIC PRETZEL BUNS

When pretzel buns are available, does any other bread even exist? It's like the fresh doughnuts on a dessert menu—we don't bother hearing about anything else, because those doughnuts are the only option. We think it's because of the special kind of saltiness the pretzel rolls get from their baking soda bath. Served with plenty of ghee and mustard or our cheese sauce (see page 44), our pretzel buns are king of the gluten-free breadbasket.

Coconut oil, for greasing

⅔ cup plus 1½ teaspoons baking soda

1½ cups **cassava flour**, plus more for dusting

¼ cup **coconut flour**

¼ cup **arrowroot powder**

½ teaspoon **baking powder**, homemade (see page 28) or store-bought

½ teaspoon **Himalayan pink salt**, plus more for sprinkling

1½ cups **full-fat canned coconut milk**

¼ cup **honey**

1 teaspoon **cider vinegar**

1 large **egg**, beaten with 1 teaspoon water, for egg wash

Himalayan pink salt, for sprinkling

1. Preheat the oven to 400°F. Line two baking sheets with parchment paper and lightly grease the parchment with coconut oil.

2. In a large stockpot, combine 10 cups water and ⅔ cup of the baking soda and bring to a boil over high heat.

3. Meanwhile, in a medium bowl, combine the cassava flour, coconut flour, arrowroot, remaining 1½ teaspoons baking soda, the baking powder, and the salt.

4. In a small bowl, whisk together the coconut milk, honey, and vinegar.

5. Add the wet ingredients to the dry ingredients and mix with your hands or a spatula until a sticky dough forms. Dust with cassava flour as needed. Divide the dough into 8 small, equal portions and, using your hands, roll each into a ball. Use a sharp knife to slice an × across the top of each dough ball.

6. When the water is boiling, remove the pot from heat. Carefully place one dough ball into the hot water for 10 seconds to coat and create a sheen, then remove it with a slotted spoon or spider and place on the prepared baking sheet. Repeat with the remaining dough balls. The baking soda bath gives these pretzel rolls their classic deep golden brown hue.

7. Brush the top of each roll with the egg wash, then sprinkle with salt. Bake for 16 to 18 minutes, until dark golden brown. Let cool slightly before serving.

8. Wrap the rolls in plastic wrap and store on the counter for 3 to 4 days or in the freezer for up to 3 months. Reheat in the oven.

DINNER ROLLS

When Laurel first cut out grains from her diet, one of the things she missed most was that last bit of bread scraping against the bottom of a soup bowl. It seems subtle, but with a radical change in diet, letting go of such dining rituals is a particular challenge. You just can't eat the same way anymore. After a few months of experimentation, Laurel was thrilled to finally have the perfect grain-free dinner roll to swipe across the bottom of her soup bowl.

1 cup **arrowroot powder**

1 cup **cassava flour**

⅔ cup **coconut flour**

1 teaspoon **baking powder**, homemade (see page 28) or store-bought

1½ teaspoons **Himalayan pink salt**

1 cup **avocado oil** or **coconut oil**

1 cup **warm water** (100° to 110°F)

2 **large eggs**, plus 1 **large egg**, beaten with 1 teaspoon water, for egg wash

1. Preheat the oven to 400°F. Line a baking sheet with parchment paper.

2. In a large bowl, combine the arrowroot, cassava flour, coconut flour, baking powder, and salt. Stir in the avocado oil and warm water until fully incorporated. Fold in the eggs and stir until evenly combined.

3. Using a ¼-cup measuring cup or 2-ounce ice cream scooper, scoop the batter onto the prepared baking sheet, spacing the rolls about 1½ inches apart. Brush the top of each roll with the egg wash and bake for 20 to 25 minutes, until lightly golden on top.

4. Serve immediately. Wrap in plastic wrap and store on the counter for 3 to 4 days or in the freezer for up to 3 months. Reheat in the oven.

PISTACHIO AND DRIED CALIFORNIA FRUIT BREADSTICKS

Under a shady tree with the Santa Ana winds softly blowing, a late-summer picnic is one of our favorite ways to dine. These delicious breadsticks are always part of our basket. Served with some vegan cheese and Mushroom 'Nduja (page 149), they're almost like a ready-made cheese board—just bake in your favorite dried fruits and nuts, and you're all set. You could even push these breadsticks to be a bit sweeter by adding ingredients like dark chocolate or candied fruit.

2 **large eggs**, separated, plus **1 large egg**, beaten with **1 teaspoon water**, for egg wash

½ cup **almond flour**

½ cup **cassava flour**

2 tablespoons **flax meal**

½ teaspoon **baking powder**, homemade (see page 28) or store-bought

¼ teaspoon **Himalayan pink salt**

¼ cup **coconut milk**

¼ cup **chopped pistachios**

¼ cup **chopped dried apricots**

¼ cup **chopped pitted dates**

1. Preheat the oven to 350°F. Line a baking sheet with parchment paper.

2. In a large bowl, combine the egg yolks, almond flour, cassava flour, flax meal, baking powder, salt, coconut milk, and ¼ cup water and stir until a thick, wet dough forms.

3. In a separate large bowl, using a handheld mixer, beat the egg whites on high until fluffy, about 2 minutes. Fold the egg whites into the dough. Gently fold in the pistachios, apricots, and dates.

4. Scoop the dough into a pastry bag fitted with a large round tip (or use a zip-top bag with one corner cut off) and push the dough to the bottom of the bag. Slowly pipe 5 or 6 lines of dough onto the prepared baking sheet, at least ½ inch apart. Brush the breadsticks with the egg wash and bake for 20 to 25 minutes, until lightly golden.

5. Transfer to a wire rack and let cool completely, about 30 minutes, before serving or storing. Wrap in plastic wrap and store on the counter for 3 to 4 days or in the freezer for up to 3 months. Reheat in the oven.

DAIRY-FREE CHEESY BISCUITS

Makes 6 biscuits

Claire collects vintage cookbooks, pamphlets, and kitchen odds and ends, always searching for the next great recipe, and recipe inspiration can come from almost anywhere. In this case, it was from the back of a baking powder can. The baking powder makes our biscuits lighter and cake-ier than traditional southern biscuits. These biscuits are incredibly tender and full of sharp cheddar flavor, with a delicate crumb—perfect for pairing with a hearty soup.

2 tablespoons **coconut butter**

2 tablespoons solid **coconut oil**

2½ cups plus 2 tablespoons **almond flour**

1 tablespoon **baking powder**, homemade (see page 28) or store-bought

½ teaspoon **garlic powder**

Pinch of **cayenne pepper**

½ teaspoon **pink salt**

½ cup **coconut yogurt**, homemade (see page 26) or store-bought

1 cup diced **dairy-free cheddar cheese**, homemade (see page 47) or store-bought

1 large **egg**, beaten with 1 teaspoon water, for egg wash

1. Preheat the oven to 400°F. Line a baking sheet with parchment paper.

2. Combine the coconut butter and coconut oil in a medium bowl. Chill in the freezer for about 5 minutes, until slightly more solid.

3. In a separate medium bowl, combine the almond flour, baking powder, garlic powder, cayenne, and salt. Add the chilled coconut butter and coconut oil and cut them in using a pastry blender or the back of a fork until the mixture looks like wet sand and the fats are broken down into pea-size pieces. Fold in the coconut yogurt and the cheddar.

4. Loosely form the dough into a ball and place it on a sheet of parchment paper. Cover the dough with a second sheet of parchment and press it into a ¾-inch-thick rectangle, about 6 × 9 inches.

5. Fold the dough over onto itself in thirds, like you would a letter. Again pat down the dough until it's ¾ inch thick, and repeat this entire process two more times. This creates the fluffy layers that will puff and add lift as the biscuits bake. Cut out biscuits with a 3-inch round cookie cutter or the rim of a juice glass. Place the biscuits on the prepared baking sheet. Form the dough scraps back together and cut out more biscuits, until all the dough has been used. If the dough gets warm while you're handling it, place it back in the fridge to firm up and chill.

6. Using a pastry brush, lightly coat the top of each biscuit with the egg wash. Bake for 15 to 20 minutes, until lightly golden. Serve warm. Wrap the pan in plastic wrap and store on the counter for 3 to 4 days.

CLAIRE'S THANKSGIVING POPOVERS

Makes 6 large popovers

There used to be a bakery in Culver City, California, that took up three city blocks. Claire's dad has recalled to us how on his ride to school, the smell of warm bread would waft through the windows of the school bus as it passed Helm's Bakery, and all the kids would let out a calm, collective sigh when they got to that part of the ride. The building that housed Helm's Bakery is still there; it's home to furniture stores now, but that smell of something freshly baked still lingers. One of our favorite baking smells is that of popovers—and they taste good, too: crunchy on the outside, eggy and soft in the middle. They explode out of their tins with joyful exuberance and have to be eaten right away. You can eat them with some sweet jam or just slather them with ghee. And if you decide to pour the batter into a greased skillet and bake it at 400°F for 15 minutes, you'll have a savory Dutch baby pancake!

2 tablespoons **coconut oil or unsalted ghee**, melted, plus more for greasing

¼ cup **coconut flour**

¼ cup **arrowroot powder**

1 teaspoon **Himalayan pink salt**

8 **large eggs**

½ cup **coconut milk**

1. Preheat the oven to 425°F. Grease a popover pan with coconut oil.

2. In a large bowl, combine the coconut flour, arrowroot, and salt. In a separate large bowl, whisk together the eggs, coconut milk, and ¼ cup water. While whisking continuously, gradually pour the wet mixture into the dry mixture, then slowly add the melted oil and whisk until just incorporated. If the batter is clumpy, break up the lumps by pressing the batter through a sieve.

3. Place the greased popover pan in the oven to preheat for about 3 minutes, until hot. Remove the hot pan from the oven, immediately fill each well of the pan halfway with batter, and bake for 20 to 25 minutes, until the popovers are puffed and deep golden brown. Serve immediately.

Notes

DO NOT open the oven door during baking. Doing so will release steam and cause the popovers to collapse.

To prevent the popovers from collapsing once they're out of the oven, puncture their tops and/or sides with the tip of a small, sharp knife. The outer structure is more likely to stay set as the steam releases through the small hole you've made.

CRACKERS
and CRISPS

Crackers and crisps are inherently celebratory. They're party animals that love to socialize with dips and cheese, especially when that mingling happens on an elaborate platter. With crackers and crisps, there are limitless flavors and textures to explore, and these recipes are quick, easy, and customizable. We love spending an afternoon whipping up a few batches to keep in a tin in the kitchen for snacking and munching.

PIZZA CRISPS

Whenever Laurel's brothers order pizza, hot sauce, dried herbs, and grated parm are always in hand, ready to adorn each slice individually. These crisps take all those flavors and toast them into savory heaven. Grab a handful as a snack, or pack them in your kids' lunches! We love them dipped in a bit of Classic Vegan Cream Cheese (page 44), too.

2½ cups **almond flour**

1½ tablespoons **dried oregano**

1½ tablespoons **dried onion flakes**

1½ teaspoons **Himalayan pink salt**

1 tablespoon **dried basil**

1 tablespoon **flaxseeds**

1 teaspoon **active dry yeast**

½ teaspoon **red pepper flakes**

½ teaspoon **garlic powder**

½ teaspoon **smoked paprika**

¼ teaspoon **dried thyme**

2 tablespoons **olive oil**

2 large **eggs**

1. Preheat the oven to 350°F.

2. In a medium bowl, whisk together the almond flour, oregano, onion flakes, salt, basil, flaxseeds, yeast, red pepper flakes, garlic powder, paprika, and thyme.

3. In a separate medium bowl, whisk together the olive oil and the eggs. Gradually add the dry ingredients to the wet ingredients and mix until a dough forms.

4. Place a large piece of parchment paper on a flat surface. Turn out the dough onto the parchment, then place another piece of parchment on top of the dough. For thick crackers, roll out the dough to about ⅛ inch thick; for thin crackers, roll out the dough to about 1/16 inch thick. Transfer the dough, on the bottom layer of parchment, to a baking sheet. Use a paring knife to cut the dough into 1½-inch squares.

5. Bake thick crackers for 14 to 15 minutes, thin crackers for 12 to 13 minutes, until golden brown and crisp. Let the crackers cool completely, about 30 minutes, before serving or storing. Store in an airtight container on the counter for up to 5 days or in the freezer for up to 3 months.

MINI CHEDDAR CRACKERS

For something to be perfectly snackable, a few elements need to be in place. First, it needs to be ephemeral—the snack needs to practically evaporate from your palate, demanding another bite. Second, it needs to be fun to eat. Crunchy, crispy, snappy texture is fun—it makes a sound and is satisfying to bite into. And third, it needs to be delicious, of course. Flavors that are bright and zippy can be enjoyed over and over again without getting tiresome. These bite-size crackers are all of the above. Whether you're looking for the perfect bar snack to enjoy over drinks or a simple lunch bag staple, these crackers deliver.

1½ cups almond flour

2 tablespoons arrowroot powder

1 teaspoon nutritional yeast

½ teaspoon ground turmeric

¼ teaspoon Himalayan pink salt

¼ teaspoon baking soda

¼ teaspoon garlic powder

¼ cup avocado oil

1 large egg

1. Preheat the oven to 400°F. Line a baking sheet with parchment paper.

2. In a medium bowl, combine the almond flour, arrowroot, nutritional yeast, turmeric, salt, baking soda, and garlic powder. Stir in the avocado oil, then the egg.

3. Place a large piece of parchment paper on a flat surface. Turn out the dough onto the parchment and place another piece of parchment on top of the dough. Roll out the dough to about ⅛ inch thick. Refrigerate the dough for about 20 minutes, until it's firm enough to cut into shapes with a knife.

4. Cut out the crackers using your favorite cookie cutter, or cut the dough into ¾-inch squares using a sharp knife. Bake for 10 to 12 minutes, until golden brown. Let the crackers cool completely, about 30 minutes, before serving or storing. Store in an airtight container on the counter for up to 5 days or in the freezer for up to 3 months.

Note

If you use a mini fish cookie cutter, which you can order online, kids will go especially wild for this cracker recipe.

ROOT VEGGIE CRISPS

Makes 5 cups

When we're creating new recipes, we don't bother throwing away the sweet potato peels, ends of cucumbers, or carrot tops. That's because Laurel is a one-woman compost bin, munching away on each little scrap. So it shouldn't be surprising that Laurel is always on the hunt for more ways to enjoy her vegetables. Not only are root vegetables vibrant and beautiful to look at, they are fibrous and full of whole nutrition, too. When paired with some of our favorite dips, they add a crunchy texture and vibrant pop of color.

1 small **sweet potato**, very thinly sliced

1 small **beet**, very thinly sliced

1 medium **parsnip**, very thinly sliced

1 medium **carrot**, very thinly sliced

¼ cup **avocado oil**

½ teaspoon **Himalayan pink salt**

1. Preheat the oven to 300°F. Line two baking sheets with parchment paper.

2. Divide the sliced vegetables evenly between the prepared baking sheets. Drizzle the slices with the avocado oil and then sprinkle with the salt. Use your hands to coat the slices evenly, then lay them out flat on the baking sheets, spaced a few millimeters apart.

3. Bake for 40 to 60 minutes, until crispy and darkened at the edges. Let cool completely, about 30 minutes, before serving or storing. Store in an airtight container on the counter for up to 1 week.

SIMPLE GRISSINI

Grissini are crunchy, pencil-thin breadsticks that are perfect in an antipasto spread. They're also a common fixture in California wine-tasting rooms, which is where we first enjoyed them. You can eat an endless number of them without ruining your appetite for dinner. We love to serve them with a variety of dips and spreads—anything that would benefit from a bit of crunch.

1 large egg, separated, plus 1 large egg, beaten with 1 teaspoon water, for egg wash

¼ cup almond flour

¼ cup cassava flour

¼ teaspoon baking powder, homemade (see page 28) or store-bought

⅛ teaspoon Himalayan pink salt, plus more for sprinkling

2 tablespoons coconut milk

1. Preheat the oven to 350°F. Line a baking sheet with parchment paper.

2. In a large bowl, stir together the egg yolk, almond flour, cassava flour, baking powder, salt, coconut milk, and 2 tablespoons water until a very thick, wet dough forms.

3. In a medium bowl, using a handheld mixer, beat the egg white on high until stiff peaks form, 5 to 7 minutes. Fold the egg white into the dough.

4. Scoop the dough into a pastry bag fitted with a large round tip (or use a zip-top bag with one corner cut off). Push the dough to the bottom of the bag. Slowly pipe 10 to 12 lines of dough onto a baking sheet, spacing them about 1 inch apart. Brush each grissini with the egg wash and sprinkle with salt. Bake for about 20 minutes, until golden brown and curling up slightly at the ends. Store in an airtight container on the counter for up to 5 days or in the freezer for up to 3 months.

COCONUT JERKY

.... *Makes 2 cups*

If you've ever made a Sweet Laurel recipe before, you know just how much we love and trust coconut. We can't exactly trace the origins of our love for this milky, slightly sweet fruit, but we think it could have something to do with the coconut jerky we used to get from the vegetarian restaurant Rawvolution in Santa Monica. When Rawvolution closed, we had to start making our own jerky. Perfect for snacking or curing 3 p.m. hunger pangs, our version is tangy, with a bit of spicy bite from the cayenne (feel free to leave that out if your taste buds are sensitive). If you can't find young Thai coconuts, fresh or frozen cut coconut meat works just as well and is readily available in the frozen aisle at health food stores.

4 cups thinly sliced fresh or thawed **coconut meat** (preferably from young Thai coconuts)

¼ cup **coconut aminos**

1 tablespoon **avocado oil**

1 tablespoon **nutritional yeast**

½ teaspoon **Himalayan pink salt**

½ teaspoon **ground ginger**

¼ teaspoon **cayenne pepper** (optional)

1. In a large bowl, combine the coconut meat, coconut aminos, avocado oil, nutritional yeast, salt, ginger, and cayenne (if using) and toss to coat. Transfer the mixture to the refrigerator to marinate for about 2 hours.

2. Preheat the oven to its lowest setting or set a dehydrator to 112°F. Line a baking sheet with parchment paper.

3. If using the oven, arrange the marinated coconut on the prepared baking sheet in a single layer. Wedge the handle of a wooden spoon in the oven door to keep it ajar and dehydrate the coconut for about 12 hours. If using a dehydrator, simply place the marinated coconut on the tray in the machine and dehydrate for about 12 hours. Let cool completely, about 1 hour, before serving or storing. Store in an airtight container at room temperature for up to 2 months.

CURRIED COCONUT JERKY

4 cups thinly sliced fresh or thawed **coconut meat** (preferably from young Thai coconuts)

1 tablespoon **garam marsala**

½ teaspoon **Himalayan pink salt**

¼ teaspoon **ground cinnamon**

In a large bowl, toss together the coconut meat, garam marsala, salt, and cinnamon. Proceed to step 2 to dehydrate the coconut.

FIVE-SEED CRISPS

This recipe is surprising in its simplicity. Usually, for a cracker like this one, you would need egg white to bind everything together and provide crunch, but instead, we're relying on flaxseed to do the same job. This combination of five different kinds of seeds creates a nutrient powerhouse full of omega-3s and other beneficial nutrients. The seeds are the flavor, texture, and structure, creating a unique and flavorful cracker.

½ cup **sesame seeds**

½ cup **flaxseeds**

½ cup **pepitas** (hulled pumpkin seeds)

½ cup **hulled sunflower seeds**

½ cup **poppy seeds**

1 cup **warm water** (100° to 110°F)

¼ teaspoon **garlic powder**

⅛ teaspoon **nutritional yeast**

Pinch of **Himalayan pink salt**

1. Preheat the oven to 300°F. Line a baking sheet with parchment paper.

2. In a medium bowl, combine the sesame seeds, flaxseeds, pepitas, sunflower seeds, and poppy seeds. Stir in the warm water, garlic powder, and nutritional yeast and let the mixture sit for about 20 minutes, until gelled (the flaxseeds will absorb the liquid and expand). Stir again and let sit for 20 minutes more, until quite thick and gelled together.

3. Transfer the mixture to the prepared baking sheet and spread it very thin, about ⅛ inch thick. Bake for 45 minutes to 1 hour, until crisp. Let the sheet of crisps cool completely, about 30 minutes, then break them up into large pieces with your hands before serving.

4. Store in an airtight container on the counter for up to 1 week.

COCONUT YOGURT CRACKERS

.... *Makes 24 crackers*

Sour is one of the most underrated flavors. While sweet and savory tend to take the spotlight, sour adds brightness, depth, and space for all kinds of flavors to exist. If you taste a dish and it feels like it's missing something, try adding a dash of acid to lift the whole thing. Kefir, a drinkable yogurt filled with fermented goodness, is a sour bomb. The slightly sour taste of the kefir gives these crackers their unique edge—and to replicate it, we're using our coconut yogurt to get that same bite.

1 cup plus 2 tablespoons **almond flour**

1 cup **arrowroot powder**

¼ cup **coconut yogurt,** homemade (see page 26) or store-bought

2 tablespoons **fresh lemon juice**

2 tablespoons **avocado oil**

1 tablespoon **Italian seasoning**

½ teaspoon **Himalayan pink salt**

1. Preheat the oven to 400°F.

2. In a large bowl, combine the almond flour, arrowroot, coconut yogurt, lemon juice, avocado oil, Italian seasoning, and salt and stir until a dough forms.

3. Place a large piece of parchment paper on a flat surface. Turn out the dough onto the parchment and place another piece of parchment on top of the dough. Roll out the dough to about ⅛ inch thick. Transfer the dough, on the bottom sheet of parchment, to a baking sheet.

4. Bake for about 20 minutes, until lightly golden brown. Let cool completely, about 10 minutes, then break the cracker sheet into large pieces by hitting it with the back of a spoon a few times. Store in an airtight container at room temperature for up to 2 weeks.

BLACK PEPPER FENNEL TARALLI

Imagine if you crossed biscotti and a bagel . . . that's *taralli*. These miniature knots are boiled before they're baked, giving them a lovely sheen and tight texture, then baked until perfectly crispy. They're a common drinking snack in Italy, so have a spritz handy for sipping when you pull these out of the oven. *Taralli* are typically flavored with a bit of black pepper and anise, but we combined the pepper with fennel and turmeric. Turmeric and black pepper have a complementary relationship—combining the two spices enhances the body's absorption of turmeric's beneficial compounds by up to 2,000 percent. What other cracker can reduce inflammation and improve digestion while tasting delicious, too?

½ cup **cassava flour**

¼ cup **coconut flour**

¼ cup **arrowroot powder**

1½ teaspoons **freshly ground black pepper**

1½ teaspoons **cracked fennel seeds**

1 teaspoon **ground turmeric**

½ teaspoon **Himalayan pink salt**

3 tablespoons **extra-virgin olive oil**

1 tablespoon **cider vinegar**

2 **large egg whites**

1. Preheat the oven to 400°F. Line a baking sheet with parchment paper. Bring a large pot of water to a boil.

2. In a large bowl, whisk together the cassava flour, coconut flour, arrowroot, pepper, fennel seeds, turmeric, and salt. Add the olive oil, vinegar, egg whites, and ¼ cup water and stir with a wooden spoon until a crumbly dough forms.

3. Divide the dough into 1-inch portions. Roll each portion into a rope about 2 inches long and ¼ inch thick. Moisten your hands with water (it helps keep the dough malleable!) and join the ends together to form a teardrop shape and place it on a piece of parchment paper. Repeat with the remaining dough, moistening your hands with water as needed.

4. Add up to 3 taralli at a time to the pot of boiling water, being careful not to overcrowd the pot. The taralli will sink; cook until they have resurfaced, then remove them with a slotted spoon or spider and place them on a clean kitchen towel to dry. Repeat with the remaining taralli.

5. Transfer the taralli to the prepared baking sheet. Bake for 20 to 25 minutes, until deep golden. Remove from the oven and let cool completely, about 30 minutes, before serving or storing. Store in an airtight container at room temperature for up to 2 weeks.

ROSEMARY–OLIVE OIL CIAPPE

Makes 6 ciappe

At Toscana, a classic Italian bar in our childhood neighborhood, Claire and her family would snap sheets of *ciappe* into warm, salty shards while waiting to order. These northern Italian crackers are large, crisp flatbreads, dotted with fork marks and flecks of rosemary. The trick is to get the dough evenly super flat so it doesn't burn at the edges and undercook in the center. All you have to do is swap out the salt and rosemary for cinnamon and maple sugar, and you've got a version of *buñuelos*, Mexican fried dough cookies.

3 tablespoons **extra-virgin olive oil** or **avocado oil**, plus more for greasing

½ cup **cassava flour**, plus more for dusting

½ cup **arrowroot powder**

¼ cup **coconut flour**

2 tablespoons finely chopped **fresh rosemary**

1 teaspoon **Himalayan pink salt**

½ cup **warm water (100° to 110°F)**

1 large **egg white**

1. Preheat the oven to 350°F. Lightly grease a baking sheet with olive oil.

2. In a large bowl, combine the cassava flour, arrowroot, coconut flour, rosemary, and salt. Add the warm water, oil, and egg white and mix until a dough forms.

3. Divide the dough into 10 equal portions and roughly roll each portion into a log. Place a large piece of parchment paper on a flat surface and dust it with cassava flour. Place one of the dough logs on the parchment and place another piece of parchment on top. Using a rolling pin, roll out the log to about ⅛ inch thick, sprinkling it with more cassava flour as needed. Remove the top layer of parchment and prick the dough all over with a fork. Flip the dough onto the prepared baking sheet and remove the parchment. Repeat with the remaining logs of dough, spacing them about 1 inch apart on the baking sheet.

4. Brush the ciappe with oil and bake for about 10 minutes, until golden brown at the edges. Transfer the ciappe to a wire rack and let cool completely, about 30 minutes, before serving or storing. Store in an airtight container at room temperature for up to 2 days.

CLASSIC OYSTER CRACKERS

N

Makes 24 crackers

We can eat these crackers by the fistful, over and over and over again. They're crisp, plain, and just a touch salty—making them endlessly versatile and especially excellent on top of a rich soup. These delightful little puffs are also easy to make ahead—pull them when they're 5 minutes short of being done, let them cool, and freeze them until you need them. Next time you need a stomach-settling snack, thaw and toast them for those last 5 minutes and you have a crunchy snack.

¼ cup **unsalted ghee** or **coconut oil**

¼ cup **full-fat canned coconut milk**

½ teaspoon **Himalayan pink salt**, plus more for sprinkling

½ cup **arrowroot powder**

1 tablespoon **coconut flour**

2 **large eggs**

1. Preheat the oven to 350°F. Line a baking sheet with parchment paper.

2. In a small saucepan, combine the ghee, coconut milk, and salt. Bring to a boil over medium heat, then transfer the mixture to a medium bowl. Using a wooden spoon, stir in the arrowroot and coconut flour. Continue stirring until a pale, stiff paste forms, then add one of the eggs and mix well to incorporate. Add the remaining egg and mix until a smooth, glossy paste forms.

3. Transfer the dough to a piping bag fitted with a wide plain tip (we used size 1A; or use a zip-top bag with one corner cut off). Pipe ½-inch rounds of dough onto the prepared baking sheet, spacing them 2 inches apart. Sprinkle with salt.

4. Bake for 10 minutes, then turn off the oven and let the crackers sit in the oven for 15 minutes more to crisp completely. Remove the baking sheet from the oven and let the crackers cool completely, about 30 minutes, before serving or storing. Store in an airtight container at room temperature for up to 2 weeks.

Note

If the dough seems too runny, return it to the saucepan and simmer over medium heat, stirring continuously, until it thickens. It will only take a moment or two.

THE ULTIMATE VEGAN CHEESE BOARD *Serves 8 to 10*

There isn't a hosting secret more coveted than the perfect well-balanced, unique cheese board. We love bringing out our favorite oversize wooden platter or cutting boards and layering it with colorful fruits, nuts, honey, and, of course, cheeses. There is something so beautiful and satisfying about the practice of putting it all together, too. The calm before the party storm sets in and the trance of readying the board can level out our stress. All the colors and textures mix just right to create something elegant, impressive, and tasty. It is a harmony of geometry and art. You want it to look balanced but still loose and inviting. Here is our strategy.

SPACE: Choose a board that feels way too big. For a group of four, you'll want a board that's about 12 × 18 inches; for a group of eight, you'll want a board that's 18 × 24 inches. Why so big? You'll need about 1½ ounces of each cheese per person, and once you slice or cube it and add garnishes, the board begins to sprawl. The expectation is about 15 "bites" per person—so when you think about it that way, you can see how it adds up. If you don't have a large enough board, simply split the food among smaller boards.

RULE OF THREE: Choose three items from each category—any more than that, and you'll overwhelm your guests and create more work for yourself. We recommend choosing three high-contrast items, so for cheese, you'd have dairy-free feta, cheddar, and parm—a soft, crumbly cheese, a savory semifirm cheese, and an intense hard cheese. When you have contrast, it makes the grazing experience more exciting for your guests.

DIVIDE AND ANCHOR: An anchor is an item you build around—usually the cheese. Once you've chosen your three cheeses, cut them into slices or cubes and divide each cheese into two portions. On your board, create six islands of cheese. We usually pick three corners and then fill in the center a bit. This keeps the board looking asymmetrical and loose, rather than geometric and fussy. Now do the same with the other categories: first do the dips, as these take up a lot of space, then the crackers, and finally your add-ons. Sprinkle over and tuck in the add-ons anywhere there's an empty pocket on the board. We like having longer items, like grissini or a cluster of grapes, falling off the edge a bit to add some drama.

recipe continues

CRACKERS AND BREADSTICKS

CHEESE

DIPS

ADD-INS

Marcona almonds

Walnut halves

Dried fruit (we like apricots, figs, or cherries)

Fresh fruit (we like grapes, figs, pear slices, or apple slices)

Escabeche

Cornichons

part three

BREAKFAST

Breakfast is without a doubt our favorite meal. It can be energizing, setting you up for an active and busy day, or it can be decadent and languid, lasting two hours over endless cups of coffee and piles of waffles (see page 115). Oh, and it's even better at night. We've developed both quick breakfast ideas and full spreads for a crowd, so you can enjoy breakfast any which way you prefer.

EPIC BAGEL SPREAD

Serves 4

A brunch feast is always welcome, but honestly, we don't have the bandwidth to wake up early on a weekend and make French toast. Enter the bagel spread—a deliciously easy solution that can be made almost entirely ahead of time. The bagel spread is all about the options; the key to a perfect version is balance. You want a variety of textures and flavors for people to make their ultimate bagel sandwich. These are some of the ingredients we always have on board.

CREAMY: You have to have some kind of schmear or spread. We opt for our Classic Vegan Cream Cheese (page 44), egg salad (see page 208), or avocado. This is the glue that holds together the perfect bagel.

SAVORY: This could be some smoked salmon (lox), gravlax, hard-boiled eggs, or even capers. The savoriness makes the bagels feel more like a meal than a snack.

CRUNCHY: Fresh vegetables bring the texture here—slabs of cucumber, a handful of sprouts, or some slices of radish will add a nice contrast against the softer textures of the bagel.

BRIGHT: Fresh ingredients that add pop are the last element to bring to your spread. We love peak-season tomatoes and peppery fresh herbs to top everything off. Some lemons for squeezing can be a nice touch, too.

Variety of 4 bagels (see page 104)

8 ounces lox or gravlax

½ cup vegan cream cheese, homemade (see page 44) or store-bought

½ cup thinly sliced red onion

2 tomatoes, sliced

1 cucumber, sliced

½ cup coarsely chopped mixed fresh herbs, such as dill, mint, basil, and flat-leaf parsley

¼ cup capers

2 lemons, cut into wedges

2 avocados, sliced

4 large eggs, hard-boiled and peeled

1 cup egg salad (see page 208)

¼ cup sliced radishes

½ cup sprouts

Serve your favorite of these elements in individual bowls and plates. Invite guests to assemble their own bagel sandwiches with the ingredients available. Claire's favorite combo is an everything bagel with cream cheese, fresh herbs, lox, and radish. Laurel loves the tahini bagel with cream cheese, tomato, cucumber, and sprouts.

BAGELS, THREE WAYS

.... *Each recipe makes 8 to 10 bagels*

2 teaspoons **active dry yeast**

2 tablespoons **pure maple syrup**

½ cup **warm water (100° to 110°F)**

1 teaspoon **baking powder,**
homemade (see page 28) or
store-bought

1 teaspoon **Himalayan pink salt**

1¾ cups **cassava flour,** plus more for
dusting

1 cup **arrowroot powder**

1 tablespoon **coconut flour**

5 **large eggs**

¼ cup plus 2 tablespoons **avocado oil**

1 tablespoon **baking soda**

2 teaspoons **nondairy milk** or **water**

1. In a small bowl, combine the yeast, maple syrup, and warm water. Let sit in a warm area—in direct sunlight, for instance (about 80°F is ideal)—until foaming and bubbling, 5 to 10 minutes.

2. In the bowl of a stand mixer fitted with the paddle attachment (or in a large bowl using a rubber spatula), combine the baking powder and salt and beat briefly to combine. With the mixer on low speed, slowly add the cassava flour, arrowroot, coconut flour, 4 of the eggs, the avocado oil, and the yeast mixture. Increase the speed to medium and beat to fully incorporate the egg mixture, then mix for about 2 minutes, until the dough comes together. Cover with a damp kitchen towel and let the dough rise for 1 to 2 hours, until it has expanded by about one-third.

3. Preheat the oven to 350°F. Line a baking sheet with parchment paper.

4. Fill a large saucepan with 2 quarts water and bring to a boil over high heat, then reduce the heat to medium-high to keep the water at a slow boil. Add the baking soda to the water and stir until it dissolves.

5. Divide the dough into 8 to 10 equal portions. Roll each portion into a ball with your hands, dusting with cassava flour as needed to prevent sticking, then form the ball into a traditional bagel shape, sculpting them into circles with holes. The dough will be a bit crumbly and may need to be pressed together to hold its shape.

6. Add up to 2 bagels at a time to the boiling water and cook, undisturbed, for 1 to 2 minutes, then flip them and cook for 1 to 2 minutes more, until just cooked through and shiny on the outside. Transfer the boiled bagels to the prepared baking sheet and repeat to boil the remaining bagels.

7. In a small bowl, beat the remaining egg with the nondairy milk to make an egg wash. Brush the bagels with the egg wash and sprinkle with the seasoning of your choice. Bake for 25 to 30 minutes, until golden brown. These bagels are best served warm, or toasted if serving the next day.

8. Store in an airtight container in the fridge for up to 5 days. To reheat the bagels, microwave them for 5 to 10 seconds or wrap them individually in aluminum foil and reheat in the oven.

EVERYTHING BAGEL

2 tablespoons **poppy seeds**

1 tablespoon **white sesame seeds**

1 tablespoon **black sesame seeds**

1 tablespoon plus 1 teaspoon **dried minced garlic**

1 tablespoon plus 1 teaspoon **dried minced onion**

2 teaspoons **Himalayan pink salt**

In a small bowl, combine the poppy seeds, sesame seeds, garlic, onion, and salt and stir until fully incorporated. Brush the boiled bagels with the egg wash and top with the seasoning mixture before baking.

SESAME TAHINI BAGEL

¼ cup **tahini**

¼ cup **raw sesame seeds**

Add the tahini to the stand mixer with the cassava flour, then proceed to form and boil the bagels as directed. Brush the boiled bagels with the egg wash and top with the sesame seeds before baking.

ROASTED GARLIC PESTO BAGEL BOMBS

1 cup **fresh basil leaves**

⅓ cup **pine nuts**

¼ cup **extra-virgin olive oil**

½ head **roasted garlic** (see page 64), cloves peeled

½ teaspoon **nutritional yeast**

½ teaspoon **Himalayan pink salt**, plus more if needed

½ teaspoon **freshly ground black pepper**, plus more if needed

½ cup **vegan cream cheese**, homemade (see page 44) or store-bought

1. In a food processor or blender, combine the basil, pine nuts, olive oil, roasted garlic, nutritional yeast, salt, and pepper and pulse until a paste forms, using a spatula to scrape down the sides as needed. Add more salt and pepper to taste.

2. Set aside 2 tablespoons of the pesto and transfer the remainder to a small bowl. Add the cream cheese to the bowl and stir to combine.

3. After shaping the dough for the bagels into balls, press them into disks about ½ inch thick. Add 2 teaspoons of the pesto cream cheese filling to the center of each disk, then fold the edges up to enclose the filling. Pinch the edges to seal, then roll the dough back into balls; do not shape the dough into a traditional bagel. Boil the bagels as directed.

4. Brush the boiled bagels with the egg wash, then spread the reserved 2 tablespoons pesto over the tops before baking.

COCO YO GRANOLA BOWLS

Serves 2 (makes 2½ cups granola)

Coconut yogurt is one of Laurel's core foods. When she was first diagnosed with Hashimoto's disease and had to radically change her diet, coconut yogurt was one of the food life rafts she clung to. Not only did it help heal her gut, but it was also a joy to eat! Unsurprisingly, it was also the first non-breastmilk food her son, Nico, ate. Filled with good fats and beneficial bacteria, coconut yogurt is a workhorse; the key is to remember to use a probiotic that doesn't contain prebiotics, which are fibers that eat away at the probiotics that will ferment the coconut yogurt. We use coconut yogurt as the base for sauces, to add flavor and moisture to cake recipes, and straight up as our favorite breakfast food. Here we feature it in a filling granola bowl. The granola contains all of our favorite nuts, plus a savory kick from sesame seeds. In true Laurel fashion, there's an abundance of cinnamon—a whopping 2 tablespoons!—to give it incredible flavor.

½ cup **walnuts**

½ cup **pecans**

¼ cup **whole almonds**

¼ cup **sesame seeds**

¼ cup **almond flour**

2 tablespoons **ground cinnamon**

¼ cup melted **coconut oil**

¼ cup **pure maple syrup**

2 cups **coconut yogurt**, homemade (see page 26) or store-bought

1. Preheat the oven to 375°F. Line a baking sheet with parchment paper.

2. In a medium bowl, combine the walnuts, pecans, almonds, sesame seeds, almond flour, cinnamon, melted coconut oil, and maple syrup and toss to coat.

3. Transfer the granola to the prepared baking sheet and use a spatula to spread it evenly over the pan. Bake for about 10 minutes, until golden brown, fragrant, and crunchy. Let cool completely, about 30 minutes, before serving or storing.

4. Divide the coconut yogurt between two bowls and top each with about ½ cup of the granola. Store leftover granola in an airtight container at room temperature for up to 2 weeks.

GRAIN-FREE GRITS
with POACHED EGGS

Grits are a hearty southern comfort food made from stone-ground corn. They're warm, soft, and so buttery that even those of us who didn't grow up on them can enjoy the indulgence. We love the texture of the real thing and couldn't be happier with our grain-free version. They're like a cozy blanket on a cold day. Just add a few poached eggs and plenty of black pepper and settle in for the perfect cold-morning breakfast. This dish also doubles as a delicious dinner side with roast chicken or salmon. Grits are easy on your budget, too—great for feeding a hungry crowd without breaking the bank.

1⅓ cups **almond flour**

2 tablespoons **flax meal**

1½ cups **almond milk**, homemade (see page 26) or store-bought

½ teaspoon **minced garlic**

1 teaspoon **honey**

Himalayan pink salt and **freshly ground black pepper**

2 large **eggs**, poached, for serving

1 **scallion**, green and white parts sliced, for serving

1. In a small bowl, whisk together the almond flour and flax meal.

2. In a small saucepan, bring the almond milk to a boil over medium heat. While whisking continuously to prevent lumps, slowly add the almond-flax mixture. Reduce the heat to low and simmer, whisking continuously, for 5 minutes, until the grits are thickened and velvety. Stir in the garlic and honey and season with salt and pepper.

3. Divide the grits evenly between two bowls and top each with a poached egg and some scallion. Serve immediately.

HUEVOS RANCHEROS

Serves 4

Claire travels to Mexico at least twice a year, eating her way across the country. And in almost every state she's visited, there's a version of *huevos rancheros.* Typically, the dish involves refried beans, some crumbled cheese, and fried eggs on top. We replicated Claire's favorite Mexico City version of Huevos Rancheros here but swapped in eggplant for the refried beans, as we tend not to eat legumes. Cooked in a similar style to refried beans, the eggplant takes on a creamy, soft texture, and the addition of arrowroot creates a thick sauce. We loaded these up with tons of additional fabulous flavors, from the caramelized onion to the different chili powders. Serve it with a cinnamon-topped mug of coffee to make it feel like a true Mexico City breakfast.

Avocado oil or bacon drippings

¼ medium white onion, chopped

½ cup diced peeled eggplant

1 garlic clove, finely chopped

1 teaspoon chili powder

¾ cup diced tomatoes

Himalayan pink salt and freshly ground black pepper

1 recipe Rainbow Tortillas (page 39) or store-bought grain-free tortillas

4 large eggs

¾ cup Salsa Roja (page 151) or store-bought red salsa

OPTIONAL TOPPINGS

½ avocado, sliced

2 tablespoons chopped fresh cilantro

2 limes, cut into wedges

¼ cup dairy-free feta cheese, homemade (see page 46) or store-bought

1. In a large nonstick skillet, heat the 2 teaspoons avocado oil over medium heat. When the oil is shimmering, add the onion and eggplant and cook, stirring frequently, until golden, about 10 minutes. Add the garlic and chili powder and cook for 1 minute more, until fragrant. Add the tomatoes and 1 cup water. Cover and cook for about 10 minutes, until the eggplant has soaked up quite a bit of the liquid.

2. Using a spoon, scoop out about one-quarter of the eggplant mixture and transfer it to a medium bowl, leaving most of the liquid behind in the skillet. With a potato masher or the back of a fork, mash the eggplant mixture into a coarse purée. Add a third of the eggplant mixture remaining in the skillet and mash to combine; repeat until all the eggplant has been added and coarsely mashed. Return the mashed eggplant to the skillet, add ¼ cup water, and cook, stirring frequently, for about 10 minutes, until the eggplant texture is similar to refried beans. Taste and season with salt and pepper as needed. Cover to keep the eggplant warm until serving.

3. In large skillet, heat ¼ cup oil over medium-high heat. When the oil is shimmering, add one tortilla at a time and fry for about 30 seconds on each side, until golden brown. Transfer the tortilla to a paper towel–lined plate to drain. Repeat to fry the remaining tortillas, replenishing the oil as needed and letting it get hot after each one.

4. In the same skillet, heat the remaining oil over medium heat. When it shimmers, add the eggs, one at a time, and fry to your desired doneness.

5. To assemble the huevos rancheros, place a fried tortilla on a plate and top with the eggplant "refried beans" and a fried egg. Finish with some salsa and the toppings of your choice. Enjoy!

Tip: We like our eggs sunny-side up. Crack an egg into the skillet and, using a spoon, baste the whites of the egg with the hot oil. This will help the egg whites and egg yolk cook at the same speed.

TURMERIC WAFFLES

Frozen waffles were a central element in the '90s-kid diet. Pop-Tarts, Dunkaroos, and Capri Sun fill out the rest of the list. Lucky for us, these sweet-or-savory waffles are delicious for grown-ups and can be nostalgically reheated right in the toaster. Turmeric is a powerful anti-inflammatory food we like to use as often as we can, and in this recipe, it's the star ingredient. These waffles are delicious as the base for our take on eggs Benedict—or on their own, smothered in maple syrup.

⅓ cup **full-fat canned coconut milk** or **almond milk**, at room temperature

3 tablespoons melted **coconut oil**, plus more for greasing

1 tablespoon **pure maple syrup**

2 teaspoons **cider vinegar**

1 teaspoon **pure vanilla extract**

1¼ cups **almond flour**

1 tablespoon **ground turmeric**, or 2 tablespoons fresh turmeric juice

1 teaspoon **baking soda**

1 teaspoon **flax meal**

¼ teaspoon **Himalayan pink salt**

½ teaspoon **freshly ground black pepper**

3 large **eggs**, at room temperature

1. Preheat your waffle iron according to the manufacturer's instructions.

2. In the bowl of a stand mixer fitted with the paddle attachment, combine the coconut milk, melted coconut oil, maple syrup, vinegar, vanilla, almond flour, turmeric, baking soda, flax meal, salt, black pepper, and eggs and beat on medium speed until completely combined.

3. Carefully brush the waffle iron with coconut oil or, if you prefer, spray it with cooking spray. Pour ⅓ cup of the batter into the waffle iron, spread with a spatula, and cook according to the manufacturer's instructions. Transfer the waffle to a warm plate and repeat with the remaining batter, greasing the waffle iron each time before adding more batter.

4. Serve the waffles hot. Let any leftover waffles cool, then wrap in plastic wrap and store in the fridge for up to 1 week or in the freezer for up to 3 months. Reheat in the toaster or oven.

TOASTED CINNAMON CEREAL

Makes 2½ cups

Drinking that last bit of cereal milk is a moment of pure childhood joy, and each kid has their number one choice—for both of us, it was Cinnamon Toast Crunch. The milk would become sweet and a little bit spicy, and even now, when we're having a sweatpants kind of Saturday, we crave a giant bowl of it. This version replicates those familiar, favorite flavors. We like to make several recipes' worth at a time so we can keep leftovers on hand for breakfast throughout the week. (Leftovers also make a wonderful crumble topping or cheesecake base.)

1 cup **almond flour**

¼ cup **arrowroot powder**

4 tablespoons **date sugar**

¼ teaspoon **Himalayan pink salt**

3 teaspoons **ground cinnamon**

2 large **egg whites**

2 tablespoons melted **coconut oil**

1. Preheat the oven to 400°F. Line a baking sheet with parchment paper.

2. In a large bowl, combine the almond flour, arrowroot, 2 tablespoons of the date sugar, the salt, and 1 teaspoon of the cinnamon. Add the egg whites and melted coconut oil and stir quickly until completely combined.

3. Turn out the dough on a sheet of parchment paper and cover with another sheet of parchment. Using a rolling pin, roll out the dough ¹⁄₁₆ to ⅛ inch thick. Transfer the dough, between the parchment paper and placed on a baking sheet, to the freezer to chill for 15 to 20 minutes.

4. Using a paring knife, cut the dough into 1-inch squares and carefully transfer them to the prepared baking sheet using a spatula, spacing them a few millimeters apart. Bake for 5 to 6 minutes, until golden brown and crisp.

5. In a small bowl, combine the remaining 2 tablespoons date sugar and 2 teaspoons cinnamon. Remove the cereal from the oven and, while it is still warm, coat it in cinnamon sugar. Let cool completely, about 30 minutes, before removing the cereal from the baking sheet. Store in an airtight container at room temperature for up to 2 weeks.

RAISIN CRUNCH CEREAL

When Laurel was pregnant with her sons, Nico and Cal, one of her biggest cravings was Raisin Bran. The mellow sweetness from the raisins mixed with the crunch of the cereal bits, all swimming together with almond milk, was a daily fantasy. She couldn't stop thinking about it from breakfast to dinner. She did what she could to stave off the craving, but sure enough, she quickly found herself making a Sweet Laurel version with her favorite natural ingredients: maple, cinnamon, and Himalayan pink salt.

1 cup **almonds**

½ cup **walnuts**

⅓ cup **flaxseeds**

¼ cup **avocado oil**

2 to 3 tablespoons **pure maple syrup**

½ teaspoon **ground cinnamon**

¼ teaspoon **Himalayan pink salt**

1 cup **raisins**

1. Preheat the oven to 350°F.

2. In a high-speed blender or food processor, pulse the almonds until coarsely chopped, then add the walnuts and flaxseeds and process until the texture is similar to chunky peanut butter. Transfer the mixture to a medium bowl.

3. In a separate medium bowl, stir together the avocado oil and maple syrup. Add the nut mixture and stir to combine. Add the cinnamon and salt and mix well until a dough forms. If the dough isn't coming together, add water as needed, up to 2 tablespoons.

4. Turn out the dough onto a sheet of parchment paper and cover with another sheet of parchment. Roll out the dough to about ⅛ inch thick. Transfer the dough, on the bottom sheet of parchment, to a baking sheet. Bake for 20 to 25 minutes, until golden brown and fragrant.

5. Remove from the oven and let cool completely, about 30 minutes. Break up into ½-inch flakes and mix in the raisins. Store in an airtight container at room temperature for up to 5 days.

SAVORY COFFEE CAKE *with* GREMOLATA STREUSEL AND ROASTED TOMATOES

Makes one 8-inch cake

A common misconception is that cake has to be sweet. Though sweet cakes are one of the things we enjoy baking (and eating!) most, this savory coffee cake is the perfect example of how our skills transfer over. The cherry tomatoes are sweet and bright, and the herbaceous, garlicky flavors of the gremolata streusel add a bright punch to the whole thing. With a crumbly, moist texture similar to a soft biscuit, this cake is especially good served warm with poached eggs, so the yolks can soak into the delicious crumb.

FOR THE ROASTED TOMATOES

2 cups **cherry tomatoes**

1 tablespoon **extra-virgin olive oil**

FOR THE GREMOLATA STREUSEL

½ bunch **flat-leaf parsley**

2 **garlic cloves**

Zest of 2 **lemons**

Pinch of **red pepper flakes**

1 cup **almond flour**

¼ cup **olive oil**

½ teaspoon **Himalayan pink salt**

FOR THE CAKE

Coconut oil, for greasing

2 cups **almond flour**

1 teaspoon **baking soda**

½ teaspoon **baking powder**, homemade (see page 28) or store-bought

½ teaspoon **Himalayan pink salt**

½ cup **almond milk**, homemade (see page 26) or store-bought

2 large **eggs**

½ cup **mayonnaise**, homemade (see page 29) or store-bought

1. Preheat the oven to 425°F.

2. Make the roasted tomatoes. Place the tomatoes on a baking sheet, drizzle with the olive oil, and toss to coat. Roast for 15 minutes, or until softened and starting to brown.

3. Meanwhile, make the streusel. In a food processor, combine the parsley, garlic, lemon zest, and red pepper flakes and process until finely chopped. Transfer half the mixture to a medium bowl and set aside. Add the almond flour, olive oil, and salt to the parsley mixture remaining in the food processor and pulse to combine.

4. When the tomatoes are finished, remove them from the oven and reduce the oven temperature to 400°F.

5. Make the cake. Grease an 8-inch square baking dish with coconut oil.

6. In a large bowl, combine the almond flour, baking soda, baking powder, and salt using a fork. Add the almond milk, eggs, and mayonnaise and stir to combine. Pour half the batter into the prepared pan, smoothing the top with a spatula. Spread the reserved parsley mixture evenly over the batter, coating the surface as best you can. Pour in the remaining batter, then scatter the streusel over the top and add the roasted tomatoes.

7. Bake for about 20 minutes, until firm and golden. Serve warm. Store leftovers, wrapped in plastic wrap, on the counter for 3 to 4 days.

MAPLE BACON CARAMELIZED ONION ROLLS

Makes 9 rolls

We love a cinnamon roll, but we need to plan our day around enjoying one. Yes, they're wonderfully gooey, sweet, and decadent—but we can't be the only ones who need a nap after eating one! We decided to create a savory version that's just as decadent but without that slumber-inducing sweetness. We love these served with eggs for breakfast or presented as mini rolls alongside a hearty soup. They're great for pleasing a crowd, too. If you have lots of family and friends coming over for holiday mornings, these will satisfy all—and no one will end up snoozing on your couch afterward!

8 ounces **bacon**, chopped

1 medium **yellow onion**, sliced

¼ cup **coconut cream**

3 tablespoons **hot water** (110° to 120°F)

¼ cup plus 1 tablespoon **pure maple syrup**

1 tablespoon **active dry yeast**

2¾ cups **almond flour**

¼ cup **golden flax meal**

2 tablespoons **arrowroot powder**, plus more for dusting

2¼ teaspoons **baking powder**, homemade (see page 28) or store-bought

½ teaspoon **ground cinnamon**

1½ teaspoons **Himalayan pink salt**

3 large **eggs**, at room temperature

2 tablespoons **unsalted ghee** or **coconut oil**, melted and cooled

1 tablespoon **cider vinegar**

Note

If your dough is sticky or loose after rolling it up, return it to the fridge to chill for another 30 minutes. It will be difficult to slice into rolls if it's too warm.

1. In a medium skillet, cook the bacon over medium-low heat until the fat renders and the bacon is crispy, about 10 minutes. Transfer to a paper towel–lined plate to drain.

2. In the same medium skillet over medium heat, cook the onion, stirring every minute or so, until caramelized, about 30 minutes. Chop the bacon and return it to the skillet and stir to combine.

3. In a small bowl, combine the coconut cream, hot water, and 1 tablespoon maple syrup. Add the yeast and stir to combine. Let sit in a warm area—in direct sunlight, for instance (about 80°F is ideal)—until foaming and bubbling, 5 to 10 minutes.

4. In a medium bowl, whisk together the almond flour, flax meal, arrowroot, baking powder, cinnamon, and salt. Stir in the yeast mixture, eggs, melted ghee, and vinegar until a dough begins to form. The dough will become very sticky and a bit loose, so work quickly. Cover the bowl tightly with plastic wrap. Let the dough rise in a warm area for about 2 hours, until slightly puffed, or refrigerate overnight.

5. Line a baking sheet with parchment paper and sprinkle it with arrowroot. Spread the dough over the parchment with a spatula, about ½ inch thick, and shape it into a large rectangle, about 9 × 13 inches. Refrigerate the dough for 30 to 40 minutes, until firm to the touch.

6. Preheat the oven to 400°F. Line an 8-inch square baking pan with parchment paper, letting the paper hang over the sides for easy removal.

7. Remove the dough from the fridge and spread the onion mixture evenly over the top. With a short edge nearest you, roll up the dough to enclose the onion mixture, creating a log. Slice the log crosswise into 9 even pieces.

8. Place the pieces into the prepared pan with their edges touching, lightly brush them with the 1/4 cup maple syrup, and bake for about 30 minutes, until deep golden brown and a knife inserted into the center comes out clean. If the rolls appear to be browning too much, cover the pan with aluminum foil.

9. Serve immediately. Store leftovers, wrapped in plastic wrap, on the counter for 3 to 4 days or in the freezer for up to 3 months. Reheat in the oven.

SUNNY-SIDE-UP MUSHROOM MINI GALETTES

Galettes look beautifully rustic and effortless and have the effect of making you appear as if you're the type of person who keeps several types of artisanal olive oil in your cupboards. It's the "this old thing?" of the baking world—a study in understatement while attracting tons of adoring compliments. This is our favorite way to bake—outwardly very impressive but actually pretty easy to pull off. The barely set egg yolk acts as a sauce for the roasted mushrooms and flaky pastry—delicious and simple.

12 ounces **mushrooms** (we like cremini, shiitake, or chanterelle), coarsely chopped

1 cup thinly sliced **yellow onion**

6 tablespoons **extra-virgin olive oil**

1 tablespoon minced **fresh thyme**

Himalayan pink salt and **freshly ground black pepper**

1 recipe **Savory Tart Dough** (page 34)

Arrowroot powder, for dusting

3 large **eggs**, plus 1 large **egg**, beaten with 1 teaspoon water, for egg wash

Finely chopped **fresh flat-leaf parsley**, for garnish

1. Line two large baking sheets with parchment paper. Preheat the oven to 375° F.

2. In a medium bowl, combine the mushrooms, onion, olive oil, thyme, and salt and pepper to taste and toss to coat. Pour the mixture onto the prepared baking sheet, spreading it out a bit, and bake for 8 to 10 minutes, until the vegetables are tender. Remove the pan from the oven to cool.

3. Divide the tart dough into 3 portions. Place a large piece of parchment paper on a flat surface and sprinkle it with arrowroot. Place 1 portion of the dough on the parchment and place another piece of parchment on top. Using a rolling pin, roll out the dough into a 9-inch round. Repeat with the remaining dough, keeping each portion on a separate sheet of parchment. Place on a baking sheet and refrigerate the dough rounds for about 15 minutes.

4. Transfer the dough rounds to the prepared baking sheet (they will all fit nicely on one sheet once they've been filled and folded). Add 3 to 4 tablespoons of the mushroom filling to the center of each, leaving a 1½-inch border. Brush the edges with the egg wash and fold them in toward the center of the galette. Cover and refrigerate the galettes for at least 30 minutes and up to overnight.

5. Preheat the oven to 425°F.

6. Brush the crust with more egg wash and sprinkle it with salt and pepper. Bake the galettes for about 10 minutes, until the edges start to brown. Carefully crack an egg into the center of each galette, return the pan to the oven, and bake for 10 minutes more, or until the egg whites are just set. Remove the galettes from the oven and let cool slightly. Sprinkle the galettes with parsley before serving. Enjoy immediately.

SIMPLE SPRING QUICHE *with* ASPARAGUS

The idea of serving dishes piping hot from the oven can be intimidating. While everyone you've invited over gathers at the table, you're hovering in the kitchen, wondering if the dish will be cooked through. But with quiche, you can enjoy the unrushed elegance of an intentionally room-temperature meal. Quiche is a wonderful blank canvas for lots of flavors, but when we were developing this recipe, our thoughts were of springtime, when the asparagus is particularly good. Served with a mountain of salad, this makes a great meal any time of the day.

FOR THE CRUST

2 cups **almond flour**

1 tablespoon **arrowroot powder**

¼ teaspoon **Himalayan pink salt**

3 tablespoons **avocado oil**

1 **large egg**

FOR THE FILLING

8 ounces **asparagus**, trimmed

4 **large eggs**

¼ cup **coconut milk** or **almond milk**

¼ cup **dairy-free feta**, homemade (see page 46) or store-bought

3 tablespoons finely chopped **shallot**

¼ teaspoon **Himalayan pink salt**, plus more for sprinkling

¼ teaspoon minced fresh **oregano**

Pinch of **cayenne pepper**

1 tablespoon **avocado oil**

1. Preheat the oven to 350°F. Line a 9-inch tart pan with parchment paper.

2. Make the crust. In a large bowl, combine the almond flour, arrowroot, and salt. Add the avocado oil and egg and mix until a dough forms. Press the dough over the bottom of the prepared pan and bake for 10 minutes, or until matte and just golden. Remove the crust from the oven and let cool while you prepare the filling. Increase the oven temperature to 400°F.

3. Make the filling. Bring a medium saucepan of water to a boil over high heat. Add the asparagus and blanch for about 30 seconds, until bright green and just tender. Remove the asparagus from the water with tongs and run under cool water to stop the cooking.

4. In a medium bowl, beat the eggs and coconut milk until frothy. Add the cheese, shallot, salt, oregano, and cayenne and whisk for about 1 minute to combine. Pour the filling into the prepared crust and layer the blanched asparagus on top, pressing it gently into the egg mixture without submerging it. Brush the exposed asparagus with the avocado oil and sprinkle with a pinch of salt.

5. Bake for 20 minutes, or until the quiche is set at the edges but still slightly jiggly in the center. Remove from the oven and let cool slightly before serving. The quiche can hold for a few hours at room temperature, or cover with plastic wrap and store it in the fridge for up to 4 days.

APPETIZERS, SIDES
and DIPS

Whenever we're filling our plates at Thanksgiving dinner, we end up with about 80 percent side dishes. Even at dinners out, we've been known to split a patchwork quilt of appetizers between us instead of ordering a main course each. We love the variety and depth of flavors you can find in appetizers and sides—yes, they're supposed to be a complement to the main course, but we made all the recipes in this chapter tasty enough to stand on their own.

MAC AND CHEESE *with* RUSTIC CROUTONS

Serves 4 to 6

The first dish Claire ever cooked for her husband was a terrible mac and cheese. It was dry, grainy, and a disaster, but Craig—a true gentleman—insisted that it was delicious and asked for seconds. Claire played along but has spent the last decade honing her mac and cheese skills to make up for that first failure. The ultimate mac and cheese is an exercise in contrasts: creamy cheese, tender pasta, and a crispy, crunchy topping. To get a pasta that's tender but not overcooked, we recommend making cavatelli—an easy-to-hand-roll pasta. It's particularly hearty and manages to soak up the cheese sauce without losing its al dente texture. Prepare the pasta the night before—or make a big batch and keep it in the freezer for the next time a mac and cheese craving hits. It finishes out any plate perfectly, or you can scoop into it all on its own.

Cassava flour, for dusting

2 recipes **Basic Pasta Dough** (page 37)

¼ cup **unsalted ghee** or **extra-virgin olive oil**, plus more for greasing

2 cups **cashews**, soaked overnight and drained

2½ tablespoons **nutritional yeast**

1 teaspoon **ground turmeric**

½ teaspoon **Himalayan pink salt**

½ teaspoon **smoked paprika**

½ teaspoon **onion powder**

½ teaspoon **garlic powder**

½ teaspoon **freshly ground white pepper**

¼ teaspoon **grated nutmeg**

3 tablespoons **arrowroot powder**

1 tablespoon **coconut butter**

2 cups **rustic croutons**

1. Dust a baking sheet with cassava flour. Place the pasta dough on a large piece of parchment paper. Place another piece of parchment on top and gently roll out the dough to about ⅛ inch thick. Cut the dough in ¾-inch-wide strips, then cut each strip into ¼- to ½-inch segments. Using your index finger, apply a gentle pressure on the dough, rolling it toward you to form a small curl. Repeat with the remaining dough segments. If you want to get extra fancy, you can use a cavatelli board (available in kitchen supply shops and online) to add ridges to your pasta.

2. Arrange the cavatelli on the prepared baking sheet, spacing them a few millimeters apart. Let air-dry at room temperature overnight.

3. Preheat the oven to 350°F. Grease a 2-quart baking dish with ghee.

4. In a high-speed blender or food processor, combine the soaked cashews, 4 cups water, the nutritional yeast, turmeric, salt, paprika, onion powder, garlic powder, pepper, and nutmeg and blend on high for about 2 minutes, until completely smooth.

5. In a medium pot, melt the ghee over medium heat. Whisk in the arrowroot and coconut butter and cook, whisking continuously, until the mixture bubbles and smells very lightly toasted, 2 to 3 minutes. Be careful not to let it brown. Slowly whisk in the cashew mixture and cook for 5 minutes more, or until simmering.

6. Meanwhile, bring a large pot of salted water to a boil. Add the cavatelli and cook for 2 minutes, until partially cooked—they should still have a bit of bite in the center and not be perfectly tender. Drain the pasta and return it to the pot. Pour in the sauce and stir to combine. Transfer the mac and cheese to the prepared baking dish, top with rustic croutons, and bake for about 20 minutes, until golden brown and bubbling. Serve warm.

7. To store, cool completely, wrap in foil, and keep in the fridge for up to 1 week or in the freezer for up to 3 months. Thaw completely before reheating.

MUM'S PASTIES *with* CURRIED KETCHUP

Makes 8

In Australia, where Claire's family is from, you "tuck into" a meal, and the "tuck shop" is a little corner store where you can pick up a snack to eat. There are all kinds of delicious treats there: lamingtons, biscuits, sandwiches, and, of course, pasties. Pasties are little pastry turnovers filled with savory meat and vegetables. Claire's mum missed them so much when she moved to the States that she would whip them up for *every* dinner party she hosted, always referencing a recipe from a stained and threadbare issue of *Australian Woman's Weekly* for inspiration. They're especially delicious with a dipping sauce, and our curried ketchup is just the thing. These are wonderful as little appetizers and can be a fun picnic snack for kids served with fresh vegetables on the side.

2 tablespoons **extra-virgin olive oil**

½ cup finely chopped **yellow onion**

Himalayan pink salt and freshly ground **black pepper**

1 **garlic clove**, minced

½ cup finely chopped peeled **butternut squash**

½ cup finely chopped **carrots**

½ cup finely chopped **turnip**

1 tablespoon finely chopped **fresh flat-leaf parsley**

2 teaspoons **cider vinegar**

¼ teaspoon **mustard powder**

¼ teaspoon **onion powder**

¼ teaspoon **garlic powder**

⅛ teaspoon **ground cinnamon**

2 tablespoons **Curried Ketchup** (recipe follows), plus more for dipping

¼ cup **cassava flour** or arrowroot, for dusting

1 recipe **Rough Puff Pastry** (page 33), thawed

2 large **eggs**, beaten with 1 tablespoon water, for egg wash

1. Preheat the oven to 400°F.

2. In a large skillet, heat the olive oil over medium heat. When the oil is shimmering, add the onion, season with salt and pepper, and cook for 5 to 6 minutes, until the onion has softened. Add the garlic, butternut squash, carrots, and turnip and cook for 5 minutes more, or until the vegetables are tender. Transfer the vegetables to a large bowl and add the parsley, vinegar, mustard powder, onion powder, garlic powder, cinnamon, ⅛ teaspoon pepper, and the ketchup and stir to combine. Let the mixture cool to room temperature.

3. On a lightly dusted surface, roll out the puff pastry to a 12-inch square about ⅛ inch thick. Using a knife, cut the pastry into nine 4-inch squares. Spoon about 1 tablespoon of the vegetable mixture into the center of each square, brush the edges with the egg wash, and fold the pastry diagonally over the filling to form a triangle. Using the tines of a fork, press the edges together to seal. Brush all over with the egg wash.

4. Bake the pasties for 15 to 20 minutes, until golden brown. Serve with curried ketchup alongside for dipping.

CURRIED KETCHUP

Makes 5 cups

2 tablespoons **extra-virgin olive oil**

1 large **yellow onion**, coarsely chopped

1 (28-ounce) can **crushed tomatoes**

1 (6-ounce) can **tomato paste**

5 **garlic cloves**, chopped

1 tablespoon grated **fresh ginger**

2 **bay leaves**

¼ teaspoon **ground allspice**

1½ teaspoons **freshly ground black pepper**

1 tablespoon **ground cumin**

1 tablespoon **ground coriander**

1 teaspoon **smoked paprika**

1 tablespoon **curry powder**

¼ teaspoon **grated nutmeg**

½ teaspoon **cayenne pepper**

¼ cup **cider vinegar**

¾ cup **pure maple syrup**

2 tablespoons **Himalayan pink salt**

Fresh lemon juice

1. In a large saucepan, heat the olive oil over medium heat. When the oil is shimmering, add the onion and sauté for about 5 minutes, until the onion is sweating. Add the crushed tomatoes, tomato paste, garlic, ginger, bay leaves, and ½ cup water. Increase the heat to high and bring to a boil, then reduce the heat to medium, cover the pan with the lid ajar, and simmer for 20 minutes, or until the mixture has come together. It should look thickened and be one deep color.

2. Meanwhile, heat a small skillet over low heat. Add the allspice, black pepper, cumin, coriander, paprika, curry powder, and nutmeg and toast, stirring, until fragrant, about 2 minutes.

3. Stir the toasted spices, plus the cayenne, into the tomato mixture and cook for 5 minutes more, or until the flavors are incorporated. Remove the bay leaves. Using an immersion blender, purée the mixture until smooth. Add the vinegar and maple syrup and cook over medium-low heat for about 20 minutes, until thickened. Taste and add the salt and lemon juice as needed. Remove from the heat and let cool to room temperature.

4. Store the ketchup in an airtight container in the fridge for up to 2 weeks.

SWEET POTATO AND SPINACH EMPANADAS

Makes 16 empanadas

Claire and her now husband, Craig, had been dating only for a few weeks when he left for South America to study Spanish. He came back six months later longing for empanadas—explosively flaky, stuffed turnovers. Craig loves sweet potato and spinach empanadas, but the filling is endlessly customizable. The best part is that they freeze well, so make a double batch and freeze a bunch for a last-minute get-together or a snack with one of our salsas (see page 150) for an extra kick!

4 tablespoons **extra-virgin olive oil**, plus more for greasing

10 ounces fresh **spinach** or frozen, thawed and drained

2 tablespoons **unsalted ghee**

3 cups diced peeled **sweet potatoes** or **yams**

1½ cups thinly sliced **yellow onion**

2 **garlic cloves**, minced

2 teaspoons **smoked paprika**

2 tablespoons chopped **fresh mint**

1 tablespoon chopped **fresh thyme**

Himalayan pink salt and freshly ground **black pepper**

2 recipes **Savory Tart Dough** (page 34)

Arrowroot powder, for dusting

Tip Reuse your scraps! If you have excess dough, reroll it, and cut out more rounds. If you have leftover filling, reserve it for another use.

1. Preheat the oven to 375°F with one rack in the upper third of the oven and one in the lower third. Line two large baking sheets with parchment paper and lightly grease the parchment with olive oil.

2. In a large skillet over medium heat, add 2 tablespoons olive oil and the fresh spinach. (If you are using frozen, you can skip this step.) Cook for 5 to 10 minutes, stirring frequently, until the spinach is wilted and excess liquid has come out. Let cool, then squeeze the spinach until very dry, setting it aside on a plate lined with paper towels. Clean the skillet, return it to the stove, and melt the ghee and remaining 2 tablespoons olive oil together over medium heat. Add the sweet potatoes and cook, stirring occasionally, until softened, about 10 minutes. Add the onion and garlic and cook until fragrant, about 5 minutes, followed by the spinach, about 2 minutes more. Stir in the paprika, mint, and thyme and season with salt and pepper. Pour the filling into a medium bowl and let cool to room temperature.

3. Place one disk of the tart dough on a sheet of parchment paper. Lightly dust the top of the dough with arrowroot and place another sheet of parchment on top. Using a rolling pin, roll out the dough to about ⅛ inch thick, sprinkling with more arrowroot as needed to prevent sticking. Using a 4-inch round biscuit cutter or the mouth of a jar, cut out 32 rounds from the dough.

4. Moisten the edges of one dough round with warm water. Add about 1 tablespoon of the vegetable filling to half of the round and fold the unfilled half over the filling. Pinch the edges together to seal and create pleats. Don't worry if it cracks—just press the dough back together with a wet finger. Repeat with the remaining dough rounds and filling.

5. Arrange the empanadas about 1½ inches apart on the prepared baking sheets and bake for about 30 minutes, until browned all over. Serve the empanadas warm or at room temperature.

MUSTARD-GLAZED ROASTED SHALLOTS AND LEEKS *with* LEMON BREAD CRUMBS

Serves 4 to 6

If onions are a shout, then shallots and leeks are a whisper. Shallots have a delicate flavor, much less pungent than onions, and sweeten beautifully when roasted. Leeks have a bright, subtle scallion-garlic flavor and melt away when cooked slowly. Seasoning them with bright, peppery mustard creates a delicious contrast against their sweetness and makes this dish the perfect side for a dinner party or topping for grilled or roasted meats.

1 cup **grain-free bread crumbs**, homemade (see page 34) or store-bought

1 teaspoon finely chopped **fresh flat-leaf parsley** plus 1 tablespoon minced **fresh flat-leaf parsley**, plus more for garnish

1 tablespoon grated **lemon zest**

⅛ teaspoon **cayenne pepper**

½ cup plus 2 tablespoons **extra-virgin olive oil**

5 **shallots**, quartered

2 medium **leeks**, white and tender green parts only, rinsed well and cut lengthwise into sixths

3 teaspoons **fresh thyme** leaves

Himalayan pink salt and **freshly ground black pepper**

1 tablespoon **unsalted ghee**

¼ cup **fresh lemon juice**

¼ cup **Dijon mustard**, homemade (see page 28) or store-bought

1 teaspoon finely chopped **fresh tarragon**

½ cup **chicken stock**

1. Preheat the oven to 450°F.

2. Combine the bread crumbs, 1 teaspoon of the parsley, the lemon zest, cayenne, and ½ cup of the olive oil in a small bowl and set aside.

3. In a large skillet, heat 2 tablespoons of the olive oil over medium heat. When the oil is shimmering, add the shallots and leeks and cook, turning frequently with tongs, until golden, about 8 minutes. Transfer the vegetables to an 8-inch square roasting pan and sprinkle with 2½ teaspoons of the thyme leaves and salt and black pepper to taste.

4. In a small skillet, melt the ghee over medium heat. Stir in the lemon juice. Remove the skillet from the heat and stir in the mustard, tarragon, and remaining ½ teaspoon thyme leaves. Pour the mixture over the shallots and leeks and toss to coat.

5. Add the stock to the baking dish, then sprinkle the bread crumbs over the shallots and leeks. Roast for about 25 minutes, until the crumbs are golden and the shallots and leeks are cooked through. Garnish with the remaining parsley and serve immediately. Store leftovers, wrapped in plastic wrap, in the fridge for up to 1 week.

CREAMED BROCCOLI
with HERBED BREAD CRUMBS

Serves 4 to 6

We don't know what we did right, but our kids love broccoli. Claire has tried to get her son, James, into chicken tenders, but he pushes his plate away and demands "'roccli." Tender from cooking in a creamy sauce and topped with crunchy bread crumbs, this dish makes the perfect side for a cozy weeknight family dinner. It's akin to the broccoli-cheddar soup we enjoyed growing up but much more elevated—and, of course, dairy-free.

1 large head **broccoli**, crown cut into florets, stalk peeled and coarsely chopped

½ cup **Gremolata Bread Crumbs** (page 248)

2 tablespoons **unsalted ghee** or melted **coconut oil**

1 cup **vegan cheese sauce**, homemade (see page **44**) or store-bought

1. Bring a large pot of salted water to a boil over high heat. Add the broccoli and cook until just tender, 4 to 6 minutes. Drain in a colander and run under cold water to stop the cooking.

2. Meanwhile, preheat the oven to 450°F.

3. In a small bowl, stir together the bread crumbs and melted ghee.

4. In a large saucepan, heat the cheese sauce over medium-low heat. Add the broccoli and simmer for 1 to 2 minutes. Using an immersion blender, purée the broccoli mixture until coarse. Pour the mixture into a 1-quart oven-safe serving dish, top with the bread crumb mixture, and bake until the topping is just golden, 6 to 8 minutes. Serve. Store leftovers, covered with plastic wrap, in the fridge for up to 1 week.

BUTTERNUT SQUASH MASH

Serves 4 to 6

It's not like we needed another reason to love butternut squash—but this recipe gives us one, with its creamy, cheesy dream of savory flavors. We've served this as a Thanksgiving side (it's so delicious!), but it's also perfect for a more casual dinner or even just alongside a simple salad with toasted bread for dipping. You can switch out the butternut squash for sweet potatoes or any other winter squash, if you wish.

Himalayan pink salt

1 **butternut squash**, peeled, cut into 2-inch pieces

6 tablespoons **unsalted ghee** or melted **coconut oil**, plus more for greasing

¼ teaspoon **grated nutmeg**

2 tablespoons finely chopped **fresh sage**

Freshly ground black pepper

1 tablespoon **arrowroot powder**

½ cup **almond milk**, homemade (see page 26) or store-bought

¼ cup **grain-free bread crumbs**, homemade (see page 34) or store-bought

¼ cup grated **dairy-free parmesan**, homemade (see page 46) or store-bought

3 egg yolks

1. Bring a large pot of water to a boil over medium-high heat. Add 2 tablespoons salt and the butternut squash. Boil until the squash is tender, 15 to 20 minutes. Drain and pass through a potato ricer into a medium bowl (or mash in the bowl using a potato masher).

2. Return the squash to a small pot over low heat. Add 4 tablespoons of the ghee and, using a wooden spoon, stir until smooth. Season with the nutmeg, 1 tablespoon of the sage, and salt and pepper to taste. Cook, stirring, until the mixture is a bit dry, about 1 minute more.

3. Preheat the oven to 300°F. Lightly grease an 8-inch casserole dish with ghee.

4. In a small bowl, combine the arrowroot and the almond milk and stir to dissolve. Add the mixture to the squash and cook, stirring, until thickened, about 2 minutes. Remove the squash from the heat and let cool to room temperature, about 30 minutes.

5. Meanwhile, in a small bowl, mix together the bread crumbs, parmesan, remaining 2 tablespoons ghee, and remaining 1 tablespoon sage.

6. Add the egg yolks to the cooled squash mixture and stir to combine. Spoon the mixture into the prepared dish and top with the bread crumbs. Bake until lightly browned, about 40 minutes. Remove from the oven and serve immediately. Store, wrapped in plastic wrap, in the fridge for up to 1 week.

140   *Sweet Laurel Savory*

CARAMELIZED LEMON BROCCOLI SALAD

.... *Serves 4*

In Florence, there's a tiny, nameless trattoria across the Arno River that serves the best broccoli Claire has ever tasted. The broccoli is tender but with smoky, caramelized edges. A bright squeeze of lemon cuts through the richness like a knife. As she devoured the plate, Claire realized how simple the dish was—it was really all about a mix of textures. We've re-created that special dish here, in all of its simplicity. *Buon appetito!*

4 tablespoons **extra-virgin olive oil**

2 heads **broccoli**, crowns halved lengthwise, stalks peeled

3 **garlic cloves**, thinly sliced

Pinch of **red pepper flakes**

Himalayan pink salt and **freshly ground black pepper**

2 tablespoons **fresh lemon juice**

1. In a large, deep skillet, heat 2 tablespoons of the olive oil over medium-high heat. When the oil is shimmering, add the broccoli, cut side down, cover, and cook until browned on the bottom, 5 to 10 minutes.

2. Add ½ cup water, cover again, and cook until the broccoli is just tender and the water has evaporated, 5 to 10 minutes more.

3. Add the remaining 2 tablespoons oil, the garlic, and the red pepper flakes and cook, uncovered, until the garlic is golden brown, 1 to 2 minutes. Season the broccoli with salt and black pepper, drizzle with the lemon juice, and serve.

EPIC DAIRY-FREE NACHOS

Serves 4

We all need a go-to junk food snack recipe, and our not-so-guilty pleasure is a huge plate of these nachos. They are perfect for sharing on game day or movie night or for indulging in all on your own while bingeing your favorite TV show. Our nachos are also super customizable: you can pretty much put whatever you want on them. The base is our grain-free tortilla chips, and our nacho cheese is the goodness keeping all the elements together. The nachos are best served fresh, but if you need to make them ahead, you can premake and cut the tortilla batter and store it in the refrigerator overnight.

½ teaspoon **Himalayan pink salt**

½ teaspoon **onion powder**

¼ teaspoon **ground cumin**

¼ teaspoon **smoked paprika**, plus more for garnish

1 recipe **Rainbow Tortillas** (page 39) or store-bought grain-free tortillas

2 tablespoons **olive oil** or **avocado oil**, for drizzling

¼ teaspoon **cider vinegar**

1 cup **vegan cheese sauce**, homemade (see page 44) or store-bought

1 or 2 **serrano** or **jalapeño peppers**, thinly sliced

¼ cup chopped **fresh cilantro**

1 **avocado**, sliced

¼ cup crumbled **dairy-free feta cheese**, homemade (see page 46) or store-bought

1. Preheat the oven to 350°F. Line a baking sheet with parchment paper.

2. In a small bowl, combine the salt, onion powder, cumin, and paprika.

3. Stack the tortillas and cut them in half, then cut each half into 3 triangles. Spread them out on the prepared baking sheet, drizzle with olive oil, and sprinkle with the spice mixture. Bake for about 12 minutes, until crisp. Remove the chips from the oven and let cool to room temperature, about 20 minutes (keep the oven on). While they are still warm, drizzle the chips with the vinegar.

4. Arrange the chips in a shallow ovenproof bowl. Pour the cheese sauce over the chips, return them to the oven, and bake for about 10 minutes, until the cheese is bubbling. Top with the peppers, cilantro, avocado, and feta. Garnish with paprika and serve immediately.

FRESH AVOCADO HUMMUS

Beans are one of the most popular ingredients in vegan and gluten-free baking—they add texture and are an excellent source of protein. But because of their high lectin and phytic acid content, which can trigger inflammation for Laurel—and many others—we don't use legumes in any of our recipes. That means no chickpeas in our hummus. To get the same creamy texture, we use cauliflower as the base. The addition of avocado brings a delicious richness to this favorite dip, and makes it the prettiest shade of pale green.

2 cups **cauliflower florets**

½ ripe large **avocado**

⅓ cup **tahini**

¼ cup plus 1 tablespoon **fresh lime juice**

1 **garlic clove**, finely grated

¾ teaspoon **Himalayan pink salt**, plus more as needed

½ teaspoon **freshly ground black pepper**

¼ teaspoon **ground cumin**

1 cup **fresh cilantro** leaves and tender stems, plus more for serving

2 tablespoons **extra-virgin olive oil**, plus more for serving

Toasted pepitas (hulled pumpkin seeds), for serving

1. Bring a large saucepan of water to a boil over high heat. Fill a large bowl with ice and water. Add the cauliflower to the boiling water and cook for about 5 minutes, until fork-tender. Drain and place in the ice water to cool.

2. Drain the cooled cauliflower and transfer to a high-speed blender or food processor. Add the avocado, tahini, lime juice, garlic, salt, pepper, cumin, and cilantro and pulse until smooth, about 1 minute. Add the olive oil and blend until the hummus is very light and creamy, about 1 minute more. Taste and add more salt as needed.

3. Transfer the hummus to a shallow bowl. Top with the pepitas, more cilantro, and a drizzle of oil, and serve. Store leftover hummus in an airtight container in the fridge for up to 5 days.

GREEK TAPENADE

Makes 1 cup

Bright, briny pops of flavor from olives make this tapenade a wonderful counterpoint to anything rich. Spread a generous swipe of ghee on a slice of bread and top with tapenade for the perfect savory snack. Put a dollop on some roasted chicken or serve it alongside our pitas (see page 38) with olive oil and salt. This tapenade is simple and versatile.

2 garlic cloves

½ cup **pitted kalamata olives**

½ cup **pitted oil-cured olives**

Grated zest of ½ **lemon**

2 teaspoons **fresh lemon juice**

½ teaspoon chopped **fresh thyme**

2 **anchovy fillets**, chopped (optional)

½ cup **extra-virgin olive oil**, plus more as needed

Himalayan pink salt and **freshly ground black pepper**

Cayenne pepper

In a high-speed blender or food processor, combine the garlic, olives, lemon zest, lemon juice, thyme, and anchovies (if using) and pulse until a rough paste forms. Transfer to a small bowl and stir in the olive oil and salt, black pepper, and cayenne to taste. Thin with more oil as needed. Serve as a dip, spread, or topping. Store in an airtight container in the fridge for up to 2 weeks.

Note

You can chop the tapenade ingredients with a knife if you prefer a chunkier texture.

FRESH AND BRIGHT TZATZIKI

Makes 3 cups

Tzatziki was a common element on Laurel's table growing up, and now it is one of her husband's favorite sauces, second only to salsa. It's a classic Mediterranean condiment that often uses dairy as the base ingredient, but our version utilizes our coconut yogurt and is the perfect accompaniment to kabobs, crudités, and pitas (see page 38). There is a creamy, crunchy, and herbaceous pop of flavor with the addition of dill, cucumber, and garlic, and it's best served alongside rich roasted meats, like our roasted lamb (see page 256), to add a bright balance, or next to a rainbow of vegetables on a crudités platter.

1 **cucumber**, shredded or grated on the large holes of a box grater

2 cups **coconut yogurt**, homemade (see page 26), or store-bought full-fat

3 **garlic cloves**, chopped

½ cup **fresh dill**, chopped

½ teaspoon **Himalayan pink salt**

1 tablespoon **fresh lemon juice**

¼ cup **olive oil**

Freshly ground black pepper

Place the cucumber in a fine-mesh sieve set over a small bowl or the sink. Use a dish cloth to squeeze as much liquid as possible from the cucumber and discard the liquid. In a medium bowl, combine the cucumber, coconut yogurt, garlic, dill, salt, lemon juice, olive oil, and pepper to taste. Serve chilled as a dip, spread, or topping. Store in an airtight container in the fridge for up to 1 week.

SUN-DRIED TOMATO DIP

Makes 1 cup

Sun-dried tomatoes remind us of our mother's kitchens in the '90s, because they showed up on just about everything. We remember the sun-dried tomato and goat cheese tarts, sun-dried tomato fettucine with creamy pesto, sun-dried tomato vinaigrette drizzled over shrimp—it was the truffle oil of its generation, an easy way to add oomph to almost any recipe. They had a real moment back then, and we're here to bring them back into the twenty-first century. To be fair, they deserve a revival because they truly are tasty. The perfect mellow balance of acidic and sweet makes them a fantastic foundation for a dip and is complex enough to serve with the simplest crackers, like our grissini (see page 86).

¼ cup **sun-dried tomatoes in oil**, drained and chopped

4 ounces **vegan cream cheese**, homemade (see page 44) or store-bought, at room temperature

½ cup **mayonnaise**, homemade (see page 29) or store-bought

1 tablespoon **cider vinegar**

1 teaspoon **Hibiscus Oaxacan Chile Hot Sauce** (page 155) or store-bought hot sauce

Himalayan pink salt and **freshly ground black pepper**

2 **scallions**, green and white parts thinly sliced

In a high-speed blender or food processor, combine the sun-dried tomatoes, cream cheese, mayonnaise, vinegar, hot sauce, and salt and pepper to taste. Pulse until smooth. Add the scallions and pulse twice just to combine. Serve chilled as a dip, spread, or topping. Store in an airtight container in the fridge for up to 1 week.

MARINATED PEPPERS

Makes 2½ cups

Marinated peppers brighten up an appetizer spread in an instant, all while adding a burst of flavor. We love adding these colorful bites to our meze platter (see page 157).

1½ pounds **mini sweet peppers**

1½ teaspoons **extra-virgin olive oil**

1¼ cups **cider vinegar**

6 tablespoons **pure maple syrup**

6 **garlic cloves**, minced

2 tablespoons **Himalayan pink salt**

1 cup **fresh flat-leaf parsley**, chopped

1 cup **fresh dill**, chopped

1. Heat a grill to medium-low, about 300°F, or heat a grill pan over medium-low heat.

2. In a large bowl, combine the peppers and olive oil and toss to coat. Place the peppers on the grill and cook for about 2 minutes per side, until light grill marks appear. Return them to the bowl.

3. In a medium bowl, combine 1 cup water, the vinegar, maple syrup, garlic, and salt.

4. Place half of the parsley and half of the dill in the bottom of a 2-quart jar. Add the peppers and pour the vinegar mixture over them; top with the remaining parsley and dill. Cover and marinate in the refrigerator for at least 8 hours or up to overnight before serving. Store in the jar in the fridge for up to 3 months.

MUSHROOM 'NDUJA

'Nduja, other than being an incredible Scrabble word, is a spreadable Calabrian salume. Yes—you can spread your cheese *and* your salami on a cracker. It's smoky, spicy, and just about the most delicious thing. For our recipe, we kept that wonderful texture and flavor but switched out the pork for mushrooms. Our mushroom 'nduja is a must for any vegan cheese board. It adds incredible savoriness and richness to anything you spread it on and is the perfect complement to a bright, creamy cheese.

⅓ cup **extra-virgin olive oil**, plus more for drizzling

1 cup sliced **onions**

3 cups **mushrooms** (we like cremini or shiitake), coarsely chopped

2 **anchovies**, chopped (optional)

1½ teaspoons **red pepper flakes**

3 **garlic cloves**, minced

1 tablespoon **sweet paprika**

1 teaspoon **smoked paprika**

¼ cup minced **sun-dried tomatoes**

2 tablespoons **tomato paste**

2 tablespoons **cider vinegar**

Himalayan pink salt and **freshly ground black pepper**

1. In a large pan, heat 2 tablespoons of olive oil over medium heat. When the oil starts to shimmer, add the onion. Cook, stirring every so often, for 30 to 40 minutes, until the onion is deeply caramelized. This takes time—no shortcuts!—so we like to make a big batch to freeze of keep in the fridge for future recipes. Set the onions aside on a plate, and return the pan to the stove.

2. In the pan, heat the remaining oil over medium-high heat. When the oil shimmers, add the mushrooms and anchovies (if using) and stir. Cook, continuing to stir, for 1 minute, or until the mushrooms are golden brown and fragrant, then add the red pepper flakes, garlic, and both paprikas. Cook for 5 to 10 minutes more, until the mushrooms are browned and tender.

3. Transfer the mushrooms to a food processor and add the sun-dried tomatoes, tomato paste, and vinegar. Pulse until mostly smooth and spreadable, scraping down the sides as needed. Taste and season with salt and black pepper. Store in an airtight container in the fridge for up to 1 week. Bring up to room temperature before serving.

OUR FAVORITE SALSAS

Living so close to Mexico means that we have a half-dozen salsas and hot sauces competing for space in our fridges at any given time. We simply can't live without it. It goes on our eggs in the morning and even into our cocktails at night (Laurel's Citrus Salsa, [page 152] in mezcal is a revelation!). These are four of our favorites, depending on what kind of mood we're in. The Salsa Roja (page 151) is great on everything, especially beef. The Salsa Verde (page 151) is perfect for pork and chicken. The Turmeric Salsa Amarillo (page 152) is an ultra-spicy multipurpose salsa that is great for adding between layers of our dairy-free cheese (see page 47) and tortillas (see page 39) for a delicious quesadilla, and Laurel's Citrus Salsa is a dream on seafood and vegetables.

SALSA ROJA

························· *Makes 2 cups*

4 **tomatillos**, husks removed, rinsed well

8 **garlic** cloves

1 small **white onion**, cut into wedges

1 teaspoon **cumin seeds**

2 **guajillo chiles**, stemmed and seeded

1 **chile de árbol**, stemmed and seeded

1 (14-ounce) can **crushed tomatoes**

Himalayan pink salt and **freshly ground black pepper**

1. Preheat the oven to 450°F. Line a baking sheet with parchment paper.

2. Place the tomatillos, garlic, and onion on the prepared baking sheet. Roast until the tomatillos are juicy and a little charred, about 20 minutes.

3. Meanwhile, heat a large skillet over medium heat. Add the cumin seeds and chiles and toast, stirring, until just fragrant, about 1 minute. Transfer to a spice grinder or mortar and pestle and grind into a powder.

4. In a high-speed blender or food processor, combine the ground cumin-chile mixture, tomatillos, garlic, onion, tomatoes, and salt and pepper to taste and blend to desired consistency. Taste and add more salt and pepper as needed. Serve as a dip, spread, or topping. Store in an airtight container in the fridge for up to 2 weeks.

SALSA VERDE

························· *Makes 1 cup*

5 **tomatillos**, husks removed, rinsed well

2 **poblano chiles**, kept whole

1 **jalapeño pepper**, kept whole

4 **garlic** cloves

½ cup packed **fresh cilantro**

Himalayan pink salt and **freshly ground black pepper**

1. Preheat the oven to 450°F. Line a baking sheet with parchment paper.

2. Place the tomatillos on the prepared baking sheet and roast until juicy and a bit charred, about 20 minutes.

3. Meanwhile, turn a gas stovetop burner to high. Carefully char the poblanos and jalapeño directly on the burner, turning them with tongs until blackened all over. (Alternatively, or if you don't have a gas stovetop, you can char them on a baking sheet under the broiler, turning them every few minutes until they are charred all over.) Let cool slightly, then scrape the skin off the peppers, seed them, and coarsely chop the flesh.

4. In a high-speed blender or food processor, combine the charred peppers, tomatillos, garlic, cilantro, and salt and black pepper to taste and blend until smooth. Taste and add more salt and pepper as needed. Serve as a dip, spread, or topping. Store in an airtight container in the fridge for up to 2 weeks.

TURMERIC SALSA AMARILLO

Makes 1 cup

2 habanero peppers, kept whole

3 tablespoons **vegetable oil**

½ cup shredded **carrots**

1 **yellow bell pepper**

¼ cup coarsely **chopped tomato**

½ teaspoon **ground turmeric**

Himalayan pink salt and **freshly ground black pepper**

2 teaspoons **fresh lemon juice**

1. Turn a gas stovetop burner to high. Carefully char the habaneros directly on the burner, turning them with tongs until blackened all over. (Alternatively, or if you don't have a gas stovetop, you can char them on a baking sheet under the broiler, turning them every few minutes until they are charred all over.) Let cool slightly, then scrape the skins off the peppers, seed them, and coarsely chop the flesh.

2. In a small saucepan, heat the vegetable oil over medium heat. When the oil is shimmering, add the habaneros and carrots. Cook, stirring, for about 5 minutes, until the carrots are tender. Transfer the habaneros and carrots to a high-speed blender or food processor (reserve the oil in the skillet) and add the bell pepper, tomato, and turmeric. Season with salt and pepper and pulse until a loose paste forms. Add the lemon juice and 2 to 3 teaspoons of the reserved oil and pulse until smooth. Taste and add more salt and pepper as needed. Serve as a dip, spread, or topping. Store in an airtight container in the fridge for up to 2 weeks.

LAUREL'S CITRUS SALSA

Makes 1½ cups

2 oranges

¼ cup coarsely chopped **fresh cilantro**

1 **serrano** or **jalapeño pepper**, finely chopped

1 tablespoon **fresh lemon juice**

3 tablespoons **extra-virgin olive oil**

½ teaspoon **ground cumin**

1 **garlic clove**, minced

Himalayan pink salt and **freshly ground black pepper**

1. Slice off the top of the orange (where the stem connected to the orange), then the bottom. Stand the orange on one flat end and gently slice downward to remove the peel—being careful to remove the pith, too, but not too much of the orange flesh. Over a bowl, slice along the membranes to release the orange segments and allow them to fall into the bowl. Squeeze what remains of the orange over the bowl to get any remaining juice. Repeat with the second orange.

2. Add the cilantro, serrano, lemon juice, olive oil, cumin, and garlic to the bowl. Season with salt and pepper. Cover and marinate in the fridge for 30 minutes before serving. Serve as a dip or topping. Store in an airtight container in the fridge for up to 2 weeks.

HIBISCUS OAXACAN CHILE HOT SAUCE

Makes 3½ cups

This spicy, sweet, tangy hot sauce is not only delicious but gorgeous, too. Hibiscus gives it a bright red plum hue that is sure to bring life to any plate. The two types of chiles round out the robust flavor and give it layers of spice that hit your tongue is really spectacular ways. We recommend literally keeping this hot sauce in your bag to take everywhere you go. Trust us!

5 dried **ancho chiles** (about 2 ounces), stemmed, seeded, and torn into pieces

4 dried **guajillo chiles** (about ½ ounce), stemmed, seeded, and torn into pieces

3 cups **hot water** (110° to 120°F)

1 cup **cider vinegar**

½ ounce **dried hibiscus flower**

4 **garlic cloves**

1 teaspoon **Himalayan pink salt**, plus more as needed

¼ cup **honey**

1. Heat a large heavy-bottomed skillet over medium-high heat. Add the dried chiles and cook, pressing down on them with a metal spatula and turning them occasionally, until just blistered, about 30 seconds.

2. Transfer the chiles to a medium bowl and add the hot water and vinegar, followed by the hibiscus. Soak until tender, pushing down on the chiles with a spoon occasionally to submerge them, about 30 minutes.

3. Transfer one-third of the soaked chiles and soaking liquid to a high-speed blender or food processor and blend until smooth. Repeat with another third, and then the final third. Add the garlic, salt, and honey and blend until completely combined. Taste and add more salt as needed.

4. Store in an airtight container in the fridge for up to 2 weeks.

SWEET BABY JAMES HOT SAUCE

.... *Makes 2 cups*

When Claire was pregnant with her son, James, she hosted a baby-Q—a fun, coed baby shower where her husband, Craig, could grill. As party favors, Claire and Craig made and bottled up this jalapeño-pineapple hot sauce. Bright, juicy fruits soften the heat of jalapeños, while adding a dimension of flavor. It's why we all love to top spicy fish tacos with loads of mango—the acidity of the fruit adds a totally new dimension. This sauce is heavy-handed on the jalapeños, with the predominant flavor being the deep, back-of-the-throat spice, so we knew layering in something sweet and acidic like pineapple would light our taste buds on fire—in a good way, we promise!

½ teaspoon **vegetable oil**

¼ cup minced **yellow onion**

2 **garlic cloves**, minced

10 **jalapeño peppers**, sliced and seeded

½ teaspoon **Himalayan pink salt**

1 cup fresh **pineapple juice**

½ cup chopped **pineapple**

1 tablespoon **fresh lemon juice**

2 tablespoons **fresh lime juice**

½ cup coarsely chopped **fresh cilantro**

2 tablespoons **honey**

1. In a large skillet, heat the vegetable oil over medium-high heat. When the oil is shimmering, add the onion and garlic and cook, stirring, for 5 minutes, until sweating. Add the jalapeños and cook for 3 minutes, or until the jalapeños are bright green.

2. Transfer the jalapeño mixture to a high-speed blender or food processor and add the salt, pineapple juice, pineapple, lemon juice, lime juice, cilantro, and honey. Blend on low until finely chopped. Gradually increase the speed to high and blend until completely smooth.

3. Store in an airtight container in the fridge for up to 2 weeks.

LAUREL'S FAMILY MEZE *Serves 8 to 10*

For Laurel, growing up in a giant Greek family meant there was a meze (appetizer) platter at every get-together. It's probably where her love of making a meal out of a lot of small bites comes from. Whether it's book club meetings, playdates, or holidays, the meze platter is an incredibly customizable option with endless add-ons that give you the chance to celebrate a variety of flavors and textures. Building one is easier than you think and usually pretty fun, too. If you're creative, this is a chance to showcase your skills by playing with colors in the form of food. We like to layer all the elements so pops of color catch the eyes of our guests. This method is as much about the visual as it is the taste, because let's be honest—we all eat with our eyes first.

Meze platters, for us, are really about the dips, so the first thing you want to do is pick out a few of your favorites. Keep them in bowls—it's easier and less messy for guests to dip. Place them around the board and then fill in the spaces around them with your bread and crackers; we recommend two types of each. You'll probably need to refill the board with bread and crackers at some point throughout the evening; otherwise, the board would just be a pile of bread. Once you've placed the dips, bread, and crackers, add one cheese and four or so add-ons. These can be placed all over the board, filling in gaps and adding color. For elements like fresh herbs or pomegranate seeds, we like sprinkling them across the dips or cheese so they have something to cling to.

recipe continues

SOUPS and SALADS

Claire grew up with her mother always simmering a pot of some cozy soup on the stove—chicken noodle, potato leek, minestrone. Claire always had a spoon ready as a kid, whether she was having just a small cup to tide her over between meals or a giant bowl with a hunk of crusty bread alongside. And Laurel truly, deeply loves salad. She craves it. When Laurel gave birth to Nico and Cal and Claire visited her in the hospital, Laurel didn't want flowers or chocolate—she asked for a salad. Each of the recipes in this chapter is full of flavor and texture and incredibly nourishing, too. This chapter is a celebration of some of our most comforting, nostalgic recipes.

CHICKEN NOODLE SOUP

.... *Serves 8 to 10*

There's no soup quite as evocative as chicken noodle. It means comfort and care on a sniffly afternoon in bed or during a quiet moment curled up on the couch. A warm bowl can cure everything from the flu to a broken heart—and nothing compares to having it fresh and homemade. We love ours flecked with bits of dill and black pepper and served with something hearty on the side, like our cheesy biscuits (see page 76). Because our noodles are freshly made, we recommend adding them to the soup just before serving so they don't get soggy.

½ recipe **Basic Pasta Dough** (page 37)

1 pound boneless, skinless **chicken breast**

1 medium **yellow onion**, halved

2 sprigs **flat-leaf parsley**

1 teaspoon **whole black peppercorns**

2 **bay leaves**

Pinch of **red pepper flakes**

Himalayan pink salt and freshly ground black or white pepper

4 cups **chicken stock**

3 tablespoons **unsalted ghee** or olive oil

3 **leeks**, halved lengthwise, rinsed well, and thinly sliced crosswise into half-moons

1 **celery stalk**, diced

3 large **carrots**, chopped

1 tablespoon finely chopped **fresh dill**, for garnish

1. Make the pasta dough. Run the dough through a pasta maker or stand mixer fitted with the pasta attachment to create long thin sheets, about ⅛ inch thick. Alternatively, dust a flat surface and rolling pin with tapioca starch and roll out the dough as thinly as possible, about ⅛ inch thick. Using a sharp knife or pizza cutter, cut the dough into ⅛-inch-wide noodles. Repeat with the remaining dough ball. Cover the noodles with plastic wrap until ready to use.

2. Make the soup. In a large soup pot, combine the chicken, onion, parsley, peppercorns, bay leaves, red pepper flakes, salt and black pepper (to taste), and stock. Bring to a boil over high heat, then immediately reduce the heat to low. Cook until the chicken is very tender and cooked through, about 30 minutes. Using tongs, transfer the chicken to a plate. Shred the chicken in the bowl with two forks or cut it into bite-size pieces with a fork and knife. Taste the broth and continue simmering until it is concentrated and flavorful, about 30 minutes. Strain the broth through a fine-mesh sieve into a large bowl and discard the collected solids.

3. Melt the ghee in a large saucepan over medium heat. Add the leeks, stir to coat, and cook until the leeks are translucent—be careful not to brown them. Reduce the heat to medium-low and cook, stirring frequently, until slightly softened, about 3 minutes more. Add the celery and carrots, season with salt, stir, and cook, covered, for about 8 minutes more, until the vegetables are just tender. Add the broth to the vegetables, increase the heat to medium, and bring to a simmer. Add the noodles and cook until heated through, about 3 minutes. Add the chicken, then taste the broth and add more salt and black pepper as needed.

4. Divide the soup, noodles, and chicken among individual serving bowls. Sprinkle with the dill and serve.

BEEF BROTH PROVENÇAL SOUP

There was a moment in American food when the greatest midcentury food minds all vacationed together in the South of France. James Beard, M. F. K. Fisher, Julia Child, Simone Beck (Julia Child's collaborator), and Richard Olney cooked, gossiped, and drank together, all the while thinking about French food in an American context. Claire is desperate for a time machine so she can go back and join one of their meals, but for now, vintage cookbooks are the closest thing. Each of these amazing chefs had their own take on beef Provençal, and our recipe draws from all of them. We particularly love Olney's addition of orange zest—it's unexpected, but the flavor is incredible and adds a citrus brightness to the whole thing. Serve this with our Rustic Loaf (page 55) to soak up every last drop.

1 small bunch **flat-leaf parsley**

6 to 8 sprigs thyme

2 **bay leaves**

2 tablespoons **extra-virgin olive oil**

1 large **yellow onion**, thinly sliced

2 **carrots**, thickly sliced

1½ cups stemmed and thickly sliced **mushrooms**

1 head **garlic**, cloves separated and smashed

1 teaspoon **grated orange zest**, plus more for garnish

Himalayan pink salt and freshly ground **black pepper**

3 pounds boneless **beef stew meat**, cut into chunks

1 cup canned **tomato purée**

½ cup diced **nitrate- and sugar-free bacon**

8 cups **beef broth**

½ to 1 teaspoon **whole black peppercorns**

¼ cup chopped **fresh flat-leaf parsley**, for garnish

1. Preheat the oven to 350°F with a rack placed in the center position.

2. Using kitchen twine, bind together the parsley, thyme, and bay leaves.

3. In a large Dutch oven, heat the olive oil over medium-high heat. When the oil is shimmering, add the onion, carrots, mushrooms, garlic, orange zest, and 2 big pinches each of salt and pepper and stir to coat. Reduce the heat to low, cover, and cook for 8 to 10 minutes, until the onion and garlic have softened. Stir in the beef, tomato purée, bacon, broth, bound herbs, and peppercorns.

4. Cover the soup and bake on the center rack until bubbling, about 45 minutes. Reduce the oven temperature to 275°F. Cook, still covered, until the meat is fork-tender, 3 to 4 hours. Taste and adjust the salt and pepper as needed.

5. Divide the soup among individual serving bowls. Top with parsley and orange zest and serve immediately.

Note

If you have leftovers, refrigerate them and then skim any hardened fat from the top. Reheat on the stovetop over medium heat before serving.

CHILI BREAD BOWL

Serves 3

More than three decades ago, on a gray, stormy beach off the San Juan Islands, Claire's uncle Bob called the Coast Guard to save some friends who were out at sea. Finally home and huddled by a fire, one of the rescued friends turned to Bob and said, with gravitas, "You saved my life. To thank you, I want to give you my most precious possession: my chili recipe." This story might sound ridiculous, but this was a blue-ribbon championship-winning chili—no joke. Bob accepted the recipe, tenderly handwritten on an index card, and gave it to his wife, Claire's aunt Tina, for safekeeping. "Tina's Chili" gained fame across the whole family, with this story always accompanying it, of course. It calls for refried beans and an entire beer, so we modified some elements to make it paleo and included a hearty bread bowl for serving. We love loading ours up with cheddar cheese, fresh cilantro, and our homemade coconut yogurt.

FOR THE BREAD BOWL

Coconut oil or avocado oil, for greasing

¼ cup almond flour

1 cup flax meal

1 teaspoon baking soda

½ teaspoon Himalayan pink salt

1 teaspoon smoked paprika

1 cup cashew butter

4 large eggs

4 large egg whites

¼ cup pure maple syrup

2 tablespoons cider vinegar

FOR THE CHILI

1 pound ground beef or bison, 85% to 90% lean

1 pound sirloin or chuck, cut into 1-inch cubes

1 to 2 large yellow onions, chopped

4 garlic cloves, minced

2 green bell peppers, chopped

2 red bell peppers, cored, seeded, and chopped

12 ounces white mushrooms, sliced

2 jalapeño peppers, chopped (with seeds)

2 tablespoons chili powder

1 tablespoon coconut aminos

1 tablespoon dried oregano

2 teaspoons ground cumin

2 teaspoons Hibiscus Oaxacan Chile Hot Sauce (page 155) or store-bought hot sauce

2 (28-ounce) cans diced fire-roasted tomatoes

1 (6-ounce) can tomato paste

1 teaspoon dried basil

1 teaspoon Himalayan pink salt

1 teaspoon freshly ground black pepper

1 teaspoon smoked paprika

¼ teaspoon cayenne pepper

OPTIONAL TOPPINGS

Chopped scallions

Chopped fresh cilantro

Coconut yogurt, homemade (see page 26) or store-bought

Dairy-free cheddar cheese, homemade (see page 47) or store-bought

1. Make the bread bowls. Preheat the oven to 350°F. Grease three 5-inch ramekins with coconut oil, or line them with parchment paper.

2. In a medium bowl, combine the almond flour, flax meal, baking soda, salt, and paprika. In a separate medium bowl, using a handheld mixer, beat together the cashew butter, eggs, egg whites, and maple syrup on medium speed until smooth. While beating, slowly add 2 tablespoons water, followed by the dry ingredients. Then add the vinegar and beat until smooth.

3. Pour the batter into the prepared ramekins and bake for 45 to 50 minutes, until a toothpick inserted into the center of each comes out clean. Let cool completely, about 30 minutes.

4. Meanwhile, make the chili. Heat a large heavy-bottomed saucepan or Dutch oven over medium-high heat and coat with olive oil or avocado oil. Add the ground beef and cook, breaking up with a wooden spoon, until browned, about 10 minutes. Transfer to a medium bowl. To the same saucepan, add the sirloin and cook, stirring, until browned all over, about 10 minutes. Add the sirloin to the bowl with the ground beef.

5. To the same saucepan, add the onions and garlic and cook, stirring, until the onions are translucent, about 10 minutes. Stir in the bell peppers, mushrooms, jalapeños, chili powder, coconut aminos, oregano, cumin, hot sauce, basil, salt, black pepper, paprika, and cayenne and cook for 5 minutes more, until the vegetables are softened and the mixture is fragrant.

6. Add the tomatoes, tomato paste, and cooked meat and any collected juices to the pan. Stir to combine, then cover, reduce the heat to low, and simmer for 3 to 4 hours, until the meat is tender and the flavors are rich and developed. Taste and add more salt and black pepper as needed.

7. To serve, use a serrated knife to cut out the center 30 percent of the loaf of bread. Make sure there's at least 1 inch of bread on the interior of the loaf so the chili doesn't soak through. Fill the bread bowls with hot chili and top with any garnishes you like.

CLAIRE'S FAVORITE TORTILLA SOUP

Tortilla soup was one of Claire's first recipe attempts. Home from college and missing the tortilla soup she would get from a Mexican restaurant that had recently closed, she tried to re-create it herself. She had fallen in love with its spice and textures—shredded chicken, creamy chunks of avocado, and a spicy broth create a delicious melody of flavors and surprises in each bite.

¼ cup **olive oil**

1 recipe **Rainbow Tortillas** (page 39), or store-bought grain-free **tortillas**, cut into strips

2 cups finely diced **yellow onions**

2 **carrots**, chopped

4 **garlic cloves**, chopped

1 dried **chile de árbol**, stemmed and coarsely chopped

2 tablespoons **ground cumin**

1 tablespoon **chipotle chili powder**

1 teaspoon **ancho chili powder**

4 cups **chicken stock**

1 (28-ounce) can diced **tomatoes**

Himalayan pink salt and **freshly ground black pepper**

¼ cup **fresh cilantro** leaves

1 cup **shredded cooked chicken** (a rotisserie chicken is perfect for this!)

FOR GARNISH

¼ cup **vegan feta**

1 **lime**, cut into wedges

¼ cup **coconut yogurt**, homemade (see page 26) or store-bought

1. Heat 2 tablespoons of the olive oil in a medium saucepan over medium-high heat. When the oil is shimmering, add the tortilla strips and fry until crispy, 1 to 2 minutes per side. Place on a paper towel–lined plate to drain.

2. To the same saucepan, add the onions, carrots, garlic, chile de árbol, cumin, and both chili powders and cook, stirring, until tender, about 10 minutes. Stir in the stock and tomatoes and cook for 45 minutes to 1 hour, until the soup has thickened and the flavors have come together. Season with salt and pepper and add the cilantro and chicken. Stir to combine.

3. To serve, divide the soup among bowls and garnish with tortilla strips, cheese, lime, and coconut yogurt.

4. Store in an airtight container in the fridge for up to 1 week or in the freezer for up to 3 months.

CAESAR SALAD *with* HEARTY CROUTONS

Serves 6 to 8

Laurel's maiden name is Czer, pronounced "Caesar." Of course, since she was old enough to roll her eyes, the easy joke—dad joke, really—has always been, "Is your favorite salad Caesar?" Well, in this case, this salad actually *is* her favorite. The first time you eat a real Caesar salad, it's like the lights turning on in a room. The creaminess of the dressing, the fresh snap of tender romaine leaves, the brightness of the lemon—it's all so much more vibrant and visceral than anything you can get from a bag and a bottle of dressing. Unlike the classic dressing, which is made with raw eggs and Parmesan cheese, ours is completely vegan; pine nuts and macadamia nuts have a subtle flavor and become incredibly velvety when blended.

FOR THE CROUTONS

2 (1-inch-thick) slices **Perfect Sandwich Bread** (page 56) or store-bought bread, cubed

1 tablespoon **olive oil** or **avocado oil**

¼ teaspoon **garlic powder**

Pinch of **Himalayan pink salt**

FOR THE CAESAR DRESSING

½ cup **macadamia nuts** or **cashews**, soaked for at least 4 hours and drained

½ cup **pine nuts**

3 **garlic cloves**

2 tablespoons **extra-virgin olive oil**

2 tablespoons **fresh lemon juice**

½ teaspoon **Himalayan pink salt**

Freshly ground black pepper

FOR THE SALAD

1 to 2 heads **romaine lettuce**, coarsely chopped

¼ cup shaved **dairy-free parmesan**, homemade (see page 46) or store-bought

Freshly ground black pepper

1. Make the croutons. Preheat the oven to 450°F. Line a baking sheet with parchment paper.

2. In a large bowl, combine the cubed bread, olive oil, garlic powder, and salt and toss to coat. Transfer to the prepared baking sheet, spacing the cubes 1 inch apart. Bake for about 15 minutes, until crispy. Remove from the oven and let cool.

3. Meanwhile, make the dressing. In a high-speed blender or food processor, combine the macadamia nuts, pine nuts, garlic, olive oil, lemon juice, salt, and pepper and blend for 3 to 4 minutes, until completely smooth. Add up to 2 tablespoons water as needed to thin the dressing.

4. To assemble, place the romaine, parmesan, croutons, and dressing in a large bowl and toss to combine. Top with pepper and serve.

AVOCADO FATTOUSH SALAD

Serves 2 as a main course or 4 as an appetizer

If you order Middle Eastern food in Los Angeles, you'll always find three things thrown in, gratis: an entire plastic bag of pita, a container of pickles, and fattoush. Fattoush is a super-bright, zesty salad—always the perfect complement to a big tub of hummus. We made this Lebanese salad a little more LA by adding avocado, and we love its creaminess next to the fresh mint and lemon.

2 **Pitas** (page 38), cut into 2-inch squares

Juice of 1 **lemon**

¼ cup **olive oil**

1 teaspoon **za'atar seasoning**

2 cups chopped **romaine lettuce**

2 cups **arugula**

1 **Persian cucumber**, thinly sliced

1 **avocado**, chopped

3 **mint leaves**, cut in half

½ cup crumbled **dairy-free feta**, homemade (see page 46) or store-bought

1. Preheat the oven to 400°F. Line a baking sheet with parchment paper.

2. Place the pita squares on the prepared baking sheet and bake for 12 to 15 minutes, until crispy. Remove from the oven and let cool.

3. In a small bowl, combine the lemon juice, olive oil, and za'atar and whisk well to combine.

4. In a large bowl, combine the romaine, arugula, cucumber, avocado, and mint. Drizzle the dressing over the salad and gently toss to combine. Top with the feta and pita and serve.

SUMMER TOMATO PANZANELLA

Serves 4 to 6

Daily bread bakers usually end up with leftover loaves—which means they're always looking for ways to revive it. Sometimes the solution is something decadent, like bread pudding or French toast, but we love a savory option. Panzanella is a refreshing alternative—the bright flavors of fresh tomato and summer vegetables accent the perfectly stale bread soaked in vinaigrette. We love this salad as a make-ahead option, because it tastes even better after soaking for a day.

1 day-old **Rustic Loaf** (page 55) or store-bought grain-free bread, cut into 1-inch cubes (about 3 cups)

⅓ cup **extra-virgin olive oil**, plus more to taste

Himalayan pink salt

½ cup thinly sliced **shallots**

2 **garlic cloves**, minced

2 tablespoons **red wine vinegar**, plus more to taste

1 tablespoon chopped **fresh oregano**

½ teaspoon **Dijon mustard**, homemade (see page 28) or store-bought

Freshly ground black pepper

2 pounds **very ripe tomatoes**, preferably heirloom, cut into 1-inch pieces

1 **Persian cucumber**, thinly sliced

½ cup sliced **fresh basil leaves**

¼ cup coarsely chopped **fresh flat-leaf parsley**

½ cup **dairy-free feta**, homemade (see page 46) or store-bought

1. Preheat the oven to 425°F. Line a baking sheet with parchment paper.

2. In a medium bowl, combine the bread cubes, 2 tablespoons of the olive oil, and a pinch of salt and toss to coat. Transfer to the prepared baking sheet, spreading the cubes apart so they are not touching. Bake for 10 minutes, or until the bread is dried out and golden. Remove from the oven and let cool completely, about 30 minutes.

3. In a large bowl, combine the shallots, garlic, 1 tablespoon of the vinegar, the oregano, and ¼ teaspoon salt and toss to coat.

4. In a separate medium bowl, whisk together the mustard, the remaining 1 tablespoon vinegar, ¼ teaspoon salt, and pepper to taste. While whisking, slowly add the remaining oil and whisk until the dressing has thickened. Fold in the tomatoes, cucumber, basil, and parsley.

5. Add the tomato mixture to the bread and toss well to combine. Gently fold in the feta and let sit at room temperature for at least 30 minutes and up to 4 hours before serving. Taste and add more oil, vinegar, and salt as needed, then serve.

6. Store leftovers in an airtight container in the fridge for up to 2 days.

CHINESE CHICKEN SALAD
with SESAME CRISP WONTONS

Serves 4

At some point in the '90s, Wolfgang Puck started selling a Chinese chicken salad at our local high-end grocery store—and it became the height of sophistication as a school lunch. Adding the crunchy wontons and shaking the container was part of a daily ritual. Soon Chinese chicken salad was everywhere—but rather than a '90s throwback, we think this delicious salad is still as relevant as ever. Every element is fresh and bright, and each one adds texture, whether it's crunchy cabbage or juicy mandarins—and we still love it for lunch.

FOR THE SALAD

4 cups shredded **napa cabbage**

4 cups shredded **purple cabbage**

½ cup **almonds**, coarsely chopped

1 bunch **scallions**, green and white parts finely chopped

1 mandarin **orange**, peeled and segments separated

½ cup chopped **fresh cilantro**

1 cup shredded **carrots**

2 tablespoons **black sesame seeds**

FOR THE DRESSING

¼ cup **coconut aminos**

2 tablespoons **avocado oil**

1 tablespoon **cider vinegar**

1 tablespoon **toasted sesame oil**

1 **garlic clove**

1 tablespoon grated **fresh ginger**

2 fresh **dates**, pitted

TO SERVE

⅓ cup **Sesame Strips** (recipe follows)

1 cup cubed cooked **chicken breast**

1. Make the salad. In a large bowl, combine the cabbages, almonds, scallions, mandarin segments, cilantro, carrots, and sesame seeds.

2. Make the dressing. In a high-speed blender or food processor, combine the coconut aminos, avocado oil, vinegar, sesame oil, garlic, ginger, and dates and blend for 2 to 3 minutes, until fully incorporated.

3. To serve, top the salad with the sesame strips, chicken, and dressing and toss to combine.

SESAME STRIPS

Makes 3 cups

1 cup **almond flour**

¾ cup **arrowroot powder**

¼ cup **sesame seeds**

½ teaspoon **Himalayan pink salt**

1 tablespoon **fresh lemon juice**

3 tablespoons **avocado oil**

1. In a large bowl, combine the almond flour, arrowroot, sesame seeds, and salt and mix well. Add the lemon juice and avocado oil and stir until a soft dough forms. Turn out the dough onto a large piece of parchment paper and place another piece of parchment on top. Roll out the dough until very thin, about ⅛ inch thick. Place on a baking sheet and refrigerate the dough for about 20 minutes.

2. Preheat the oven to 400°F.

3. Remove the dough from the fridge and cut it into ¼-inch-wide strips, about 2 to 3 inches long. Place the strips on the parchment paper on the baking sheet, spacing them 1 inch apart. Bake for 15 minutes, or until golden brown. Remove from the oven and let cool. Store in an airtight container on the counter for up to 1 week.

WATERMELON CRISPY PITA BOWL

We dare you to find a recipe that screams "summertime" more than this one! Claire's absolute favorite summer treat is watermelon—one Fourth of July, she ate an entire melon in a single sitting. Watermelon is often thought of as just a simple snack or dessert, but why can't you create a dinner dish around this juicy fruit? You can. Aromatic lemon and mint bring a bright note to the feta and pistachio. This dish is surprising, comforting, and refreshing all at once.

2 **Pitas** (page 38), cut into 2-inch squares

1 **watermelon**, cut into 1-inch cubes

1 cup crumbled **dairy-free feta**, homemade (see page 46) or store-bought

½ cup **pistachios**, coarsely chopped

4 or 5 **mint** leaves

2 tablespoons **extra-virgin olive oil**

1 tablespoon **fresh lemon juice**

Pinch of **Himalayan pink salt**

1. Preheat the oven to 400°F. Line a baking sheet with parchment paper.

2. Place the pita squares on the prepared baking sheet, spacing them apart, and bake for 12 to 15 minutes, until crispy. Remove from the oven and let cool.

3. In a large bowl, combine the watermelon, feta, pistachios, toasted pita squares, and mint.

4. In a small bowl, whisk together the olive oil, lemon juice, and salt until fully incorporated. Add the dressing to the watermelon mixture and toss to coat. Serve immediately.

ROASTED VEGGIE BOWL *with* GREEN GODDESS DRESSING AND GREMOLATA BREAD CRUMBS

Serves 4 to 6

One of the best things about this veggie bowl is that all the elements can be made ahead. We love to spend our Sunday afternoons prepping it for easy weekday lunches. Not only do the components sing together in this recipe, but they can also all be used in other meals throughout the week! The dressing is delicious on a quinoa salad, the bread crumbs can be used to top a vegetable frittata for some extra crunch, and the vegetables can be tossed in with any grilled protein for a lean dinner.

1 head **cauliflower**, cut into florets

1 pound **Brussels sprouts**, halved

1 head **broccoli**, cut into florets

1 large **sweet potato**, peeled and chopped into 1-inch pieces

1 large **shallot**, chopped

2 tablespoons **avocado oil**

1 teaspoon **Himalayan pink salt**

2 cups **arugula**

1 cup **Green Goddess Dressing** (recipe follows)

Gremolata Bread Crumbs (page 248)

1. Preheat the oven to 400°F. Line a baking sheet with parchment paper.

2. In a large bowl, combine the cauliflower, Brussels sprouts, broccoli, sweet potato, shallot, avocado oil, and salt and toss to coat. Arrange the vegetables on the prepared baking sheet, spacing them so they are not touching or overlapping, and bake for 40 minutes, or until browned at the edges. Remove from the baking sheet and let cool.

3. In a large bowl, combine the roasted vegetables, arugula, dressing, and bread crumbs and toss to combine. Serve.

GREEN GODDESS DRESSING

½ ripe large **avocado**

¼ cup **olive oil** or **avocado oil**

2½ tablespoons **fresh lemon juice**

2 **garlic cloves**

½ teaspoon **Himalayan pink salt**

1 tablespoon fresh tarragon leaves

1½ tablespoons chopped **fresh chives**

½ cup roughly chopped fresh **flat-leaf parsley**

½ cup **watercress** or **spinach**

In a high-speed blender or food processor, combine the avocado, olive oil, lemon juice, garlic, salt, tarragon, chives, parsley, and watercress and blend for 2 to 3 minutes, until smooth. Add water as needed to get desired texture. Store in an airtight container in the fridge for up to 4 days.

Soups and Salads 183

It's hard to hear "sandwich" and not think of the brown paper lunch sack many of us toted in hand when we went off to grade school in the morning. (Okay, or maybe you used a pink princess lunch box.) But there can be so much more between the bread than some cold cuts. For us, the bread is the perfect canvas to let your creativity fly, from fillings to toppings to condiments. Don't be afraid to add all the little oddball items in your fridge to some of these recipes; they only get better the more you experiment.

SANDWICHES

THE ULTIMATE SWEET LAUREL BURGER
with SWEET POTATO FRIES

Serves 4

Los Angeles is a burger town—between the Tommy's, Tomy's, and Thom's dotting street corners all over the Westside, you can hardly go a few blocks without bumping into a classic burger spot. Our favorite burger is the one served at the Apple Pan, a diner where they haven't changed any recipes since 1949. Our parents and grandparents all used to visit Apple Pan, too. The classic "LA burger" is a crispy-edged masterpiece with rich, savory flavors, which is exactly what inspired this version.

FOR THE SWEET POTATO FRIES

4 pounds **sweet potatoes**, halved and cut into ¼-inch-thick strips

¼ cup **coconut oil**, melted, or **avocado oil**

2 tablespoons **cider vinegar**

1 to 2 tablespoons **Italian seasoning**

1 to 2 teaspoons **garlic powder**

1 tablespoon **Himalayan pink salt**

¼ teaspoon **cayenne pepper**

FOR THE BURGERS

1 pound **ground beef chuck** (beef shoulder, 80% lean), bison, beef, turkey, lamb, or chicken, or a mix

1 tablespoon **garlic powder**

1 teaspoon **Himalayan pink salt**

1 teaspoon **freshly ground black pepper**

1 teaspoon **ground cumin**

¼ teaspoon **cayenne pepper**

Avocado oil, for greasing

4 slices dairy-free **cheddar cheese**, homemade (see page 47) or store-bought (optional)

4 **Sesame-Studded Burger Buns** (page 69) or store-bought buns

Ketchup

4 slices **tomato** (optional)

4 **butter lettuce leaves** (optional)

1. Make the fries. Preheat the oven to 425°F. Line a baking sheet with parchment paper.

2. In a large bowl, combine the potatoes, coconut oil, vinegar, Italian seasoning, garlic powder, salt, and cayenne and toss to coat. Transfer to the prepared baking sheet and arrange in an even layer. Bake for 40 minutes, flipping the fries once halfway through, until golden brown.

3. In a large bowl, combine the ground meat, garlic powder, salt, black pepper, cumin, and cayenne and mix with your hands until just combined. Form the mixture into 4 patties, using about ¼ cup of the mixture for each, and press them to about 4 inches wide (ragged edges are your friend!).

4. Heat a large skillet over medium-high heat for about 2 minutes, until very hot. Coat the pan lightly with avocado oil. Add the patties and cook, pressing down on them with a metal spatula a few times to get a nice sear, for about 3 minutes per side for medium. If you're making cheeseburgers, add the cheese after you flip the patties so the cheese melts as the patty cooks.

5. Place each patty on a bun and top with ketchup, a tomato slice, and lettuce, if desired, and close the buns. Serve with the sweet potato fries alongside.

Note

If you're using ground bison, turkey, or chicken, add 2 tablespoons avocado oil to the ground meat mixture before forming the patties.

OUR FAVORITE VEGAN BURGER

Makes 6 burgers

Vegan burgers and the grain-free lifestyle don't usually go hand in hand, since they're often loaded with legumes and other starchy items. We decided to make an all-veggie burger filled only with paleo-approved vegetables like sweet potatoes, mushrooms, and zucchini. We love serving this up with a side of our delicious ketchup and some fries, but you could also serve the patty on a bed of lettuce with our Green Goddess Dressing (page 183).

1 tablespoon **avocado oil**

1½ cups chopped **mushrooms**

¼ medium **yellow onion**, finely chopped

1 medium **carrot**, finely chopped

½ medium **zucchini**, finely chopped

½ medium **sweet potato**, peeled and finely chopped

1 **garlic clove**, minced

¼ cup **almond flour**

1 tablespoon **flax meal**

½ teaspoon **ground cumin**

1½ teaspoons **tomato paste**

½ teaspoon **Himalayan pink salt**

¼ teaspoon **freshly ground black pepper**

6 **vegan pretzel buns**

OPTIONAL TOPPINGS

2 **avocados**, sliced

6 slices **dairy-free cheddar cheese**, homemade (see page 47) or store-bought

6 slices **red onion**

6 slices **heirloom tomato**

Ketchup

1. Preheat the oven to 400°F. Line a baking sheet with parchment paper.

2. In a large skillet, heat the avocado oil over medium heat. When the oil is shimmering, add the mushrooms, onion, carrot, and zucchini and cook, stirring, for about 5 minutes, until just tender. Add the sweet potato and garlic and cook for 5 minutes more, or until lightly golden brown and tender. Take the pan off the heat and let the vegetables cool for about 5 minutes, just long enough that they're not piping hot.

3. Transfer the sautéed vegetables to a food processor and pulse until finely chopped but not puréed. Transfer the mixture to a large bowl. Add the almond flour, flax meal, cumin, tomato paste, salt, and pepper and mix well using your hands. Form the mixture into 6 patties and place them on the prepared baking sheet.

4. Bake for 15 minutes, then carefully flip the patties and bake for 15 minutes more, or until golden brown. Remove the pan from the oven and let the patties cool slightly.

5. Place each patty on a bun and top with avocado, cheddar cheese, onion, a tomato slice, and ketchup, if desired, and close the buns.

ROASTED CAULIFLOWER STEAK SANDWICH

Makes 4 sandwiches

Cauliflower recently became a favorite vegetable of ours for its versatility. It can be used as "rice" or "mashed potatoes," but we love it best served as a main course, especially between two slices of delicious bread with BBQ sauce and tons of peppery arugula. The phrase "cauliflower steak" is so appealing to us. A thick veggie slab, completely tender and caramelized to enhance its sweetness and nuttiness. The trick with cauliflower steaks is to make sure you're keeping an eye on them during roasting—if they go too long, they'll be totally overdone and turn to mush.

1 head **cauliflower**, cut vertically into 2-inch-thick slices

3 tablespoons **avocado oil**

1 teaspoon **smoked paprika**

¼ teaspoon **Himalayan pink salt**

¼ cup homemade **BBQ sauce** (recipe follows), or store-bought

8 slices **Perfect Sandwich Bread** (page 56), or 4 Dinner Rolls (page 72)

2 cups **arugula**

1. Preheat the oven to 400°F. Line a baking sheet with parchment paper.

2. Place the cauliflower slices on the prepared baking sheet, coat all over with the avocado oil, paprika, and salt and bake for 25 minutes, then flip and bake for 15 minutes more, or until golden brown. Remove from the oven and let cool completely, about 20 minutes.

3. Spread the BBQ sauce on one side of each slice of bread. Place a cauliflower steak on 4 of the slices, top with arugula, and close the sandwiches with the second slice of bread.

MAPLE BBQ SAUCE

⅔ cup ketchup (see page 133)

½ cup cider vinegar

½ cup maple syrup

2 teaspoons smoked paprika

1 teaspoon ground cumin

1 teaspoon Himalayan salt

1 teaspoon freshly ground black pepper

1 (14-ounce) can peaches in juice (not syrup), juice strained, or 1 cup fresh peaches, peeled and sliced

In a medium sized saucepan over medium heat, combine the ketchup, vinegar, maple syrup, paprika, cumin, salt, black pepper, and peaches and bring to a simmer. Cook for 5 minutes, stirring occasionally. Blend until totally smooth. Store in an airtight container in the fridge for up to 1 month.

HUSBAND BBQ

Have you ever met a barbecue nerd? The kind of person who can tell you, definitively, the best rub, the best wood for smoke, the best method for succulent brisket, and the best BBQ joint in the country? (It's Central BBQ in Memphis, by the way.) That's Claire's husband, Craig; any time he cooks, it's barbecue. This recipe is inspired by his go-to method for pulled pork, the base for the most delicious sandwiches. We dare say it could rival some of the best barbecue joints in the South.

FOR THE PULLED PORK

½ teaspoon **freshly ground black pepper**

2 teaspoons coarse **Himalayan pink salt**

1 tablespoon **maple sugar, coconut sugar, or pure maple syrup**

½ teaspoon **mustard powder**

1½ teaspoons **chili powder**

2 pounds **boneless pork shoulder**

¼ cup **pure maple syrup**

1 cup **Maple BBQ Sauce** (page 190)

FOR THE SLAW

1 **garlic clove**, minced

½ cup **mayonnaise**, homemade (see page 29) or store-bought

1 tablespoon **Sweet Baby James Hot Sauce** (page 156) or store-bought hot sauce, plus more for serving

3 tablespoons **cider vinegar**

2 tablespoons **pure maple syrup** or **honey**

4 cups thinly sliced **cabbage**

¼ cup thinly sliced **jalapeño peppers**

¼ cup finely chopped **fresh flat-leaf parsley**

¼ cup **scallions**, green and white parts thinly sliced

8 **Dinner Rolls** (page 72)

½ cup **unsalted ghee**, melted (optional)

1. Make the pork. In a small bowl, combine the pepper, salt, maple sugar, mustard powder, and chili powder. Rub the spice mixture all over the pork, cover with plastic wrap, and let rest at room temperature for 1 to 2 hours or refrigerate for at least 3 hours or up to overnight.

2. Preheat the oven to 300°F.

3. Place the marinated pork in a large roasting pan and roast for 3 to 4 hours, until the meat is tender and falling apart and a thermometer inserted into the thickest part reads 200°F. Remove the pork from the oven and increase the oven temperature to 500°F. Brush the pork with the maple syrup and return it to the oven. Roast until the maple syrup is bubbling and forms a caramel crust on the pork, about 10 minutes. Remove from the oven and let cool for at least 30 minutes, then shred the pork with tongs or two forks. Add the BBQ sauce and toss to coat, adding more sauce as needed.

4. Make the slaw. In a medium bowl, whisk together the garlic, mayonnaise, hot sauce, vinegar, and maple syrup. Add the cabbage, jalapeños, parsley, and scallions and toss to coat.

5. Split the buns and brush the inside with the melted ghee, if desired. Top the bottom half of each bun with pulled pork and slaw and close the buns. Serve with extra hot sauce, if desired.

Note

We like to heat up the buns a bit by popping them in the microwave for about 10 seconds before brushing them with ghee.

NO-GARBANZO FALAFEL

In Paris, there is a street with two warring falafel spots: L'As du Fallafel and Mi-Va-Mi. Both are Israeli-style, with crisp falafel tucked into soft pita and loaded with fresh vegetables, pickles, and sauces—and both are delicious. If you're a local, you have your favorite and will defend it with your life. As outsiders, we don't pick sides, so we drew inspiration from both to create our paleo version, without chickpeas. This means tons of fresh herbs and spices in the falafel mixture and in the garnishes.

¼ **cauliflower head**, minced (about 2 cups)

2 **garlic cloves**, minced

½ cup grated **yellow onion**

¼ cup chopped **fresh cilantro**

¼ cup chopped **fresh flat-leaf parsley**

½ teaspoon **Himalayan pink salt**

1 large **egg**

2 tablespoons **arrowroot powder**, plus more for dusting

1 teaspoon **ground cumin**

½ teaspoon **ground coriander**

½ teaspoon **freshly ground black pepper**

¼ teaspoon **cayenne pepper**

Pinch of **ground cardamom**

½ teaspoon **baking powder**, homemade (see page 28) or store-bought

Avocado oil or **coconut oil**, for frying

Pitas (page 38), for serving (optional)

OPTIONAL TOPPINGS

½ cup **tzatziki**, homemade (see page 147) or store-bought

1 bunch **cilantro**, coarsely chopped

1 large **thin-skinned cucumber**, cut into thin strips

1 tablespoon **toasted sesame seeds**

1 cup **Fermented Cabbage** (page 203) or store-bought (such as sauerkraut or kimchi)

Hibiscus Oaxacan Chile Hot Sauce (page 155) or store-bought hot sauce

1. In a food processor, combine the cauliflower, garlic, onion, cilantro, parsley, salt, egg, arrowroot, cumin, coriander, black pepper, cayenne, cardamom, and baking powder. Pulse until a rough, coarse meal forms; it should be slightly dry and crumbly but holding together. Transfer the mixture to a large bowl, cover with plastic wrap, and refrigerate for at least 1 hour or up to overnight.

2. With wet hands, form the falafel mixture into roughly 1-inch balls, then lightly dust them with arrowroot.

3. Fill a deep medium skillet with avocado oil to a depth of 1½ inches. Attach a deep-fry thermometer to the side and heat the oil over medium to 375°F. Test one falafel by carefully dropping it into the hot oil. Working in small batches, fry the falafel for 2 to 3 minutes per side, until golden brown. Transfer to a paper towel–lined plate to drain.

4. Enjoy the falafel on its own or stuffed into a pita with tzatziki, cilantro, cucumber, sesame seeds, fermented cabbage, and hot sauce, as desired.

THE BEST VEGAN BLT

Makes 1 sandwich

If Laurel and Claire were ever to come to blows over food, it would be over bacon. Claire loves it, Laurel does not. But Laurel is surprisingly strong and won the deciding arm-wrestling contest, so here we are with a vegan bacon that even Claire thinks is delicious. When you toast coconut with spices, coconut aminos, and a little maple syrup, you get a deeply savory, sweet, and smoky crunch that we love. No, it doesn't sizzle like the real stuff, but it's a perfect stand-in in this sandwich. If you have leftover coconut bacon, you can crumble it over salads, include it in trail mix, or just enjoy it as a snack.

FOR THE COCONUT BACON

1 tablespoon **arrowroot powder**

½ cup **hot water** (110° to 120°F)

2 cups unsweetened large **coconut flakes**

1 tablespoon **coconut oil**, melted

2 tablespoons **coconut aminos**

1 teaspoon **smoked paprika**

1 tablespoon **pure maple syrup**

Pinch of **Himalayan pink salt** or smoked sea salt

½ teaspoon **freshly ground black pepper**

FOR THE SANDWICH

2 **Classic Pretzel Buns** (page 71) or **Dairy-Free Cheddar Biscuits** (page 76, without egg wash for vegan option)

1 **garlic clove**, halved

1 tablespoon **vegan aioli**, homemade (see page 29) or store-bought

Himalayan pink salt and **freshly ground black pepper**

2 slices **heirloom tomato**, about ¼ inch thick each

1 **butter lettuce leaf**

1. Make the bacon. Preheat the oven to 325°F. Line a baking sheet with parchment paper.

2. In a large bowl, combine the arrowroot and hot water, stirring until the arrowroot dissolves. Add the coconut flakes, coconut oil, coconut aminos, paprika, maple syrup, salt, and pepper and toss to coat.

3. Form the mixture into ten 1-inch-wide strips on the prepared baking sheet, spacing them apart so there's no overlapping. Bake for 6 minutes, then flip the strips, rotate the pan, and bake for 5 to 7 minutes more, until the coconut bacon is crispy and golden brown, being careful not to burn it. Remove from the oven and let cool for 15 minutes. Store in an airtight container at room temperature for up to 1 week or in the freezer for up to 1 month.

4. Assemble the sandwiches. Rub each bun all over with half a garlic clove. Spread the aioli on one side of each slice and season with salt and pepper. Top one bun with the tomato, lettuce, Coconut Bacon, and the second bun to finish.

5. Slice diagonally and serve.

SANTA MONICA GRILLED FISH TACOS

Makes 4 tacos

Lifeguards in the summer, surfers when the waves are big, and spear-divers when the halibut come in—Laurel's five brothers are basically varying versions of Aquaman. So depending on the season, that means fish tacos every weekend. We love them with halibut or white sea bass, as fresh as you can find it, and served with a spicy slaw. Ours is slightly spicy, tangy, and crunchy. When we're hungry after a long day at the beach, this is always our go-to.

1 head **green cabbage**, thinly sliced

2 **shallots**, chopped

1 **serrano pepper**, chopped

⅓ cup chopped **fresh cilantro**

¼ cup plus 2 tablespoons **avocado oil**, plus more for grilling

1¼ teaspoons **Himalayan pink salt**

1 pound **halibut** or **white sea bass**, cut into 4 pieces

1 teaspoon **smoked paprika**

¼ teaspoon **garlic powder**

1 recipe **Rainbow Tortillas** (page 39) or store-bought grain-free tortillas, warmed

OPTIONAL TOPPINGS

1 **lime**, cut into wedges

½ cup coarsely chopped **fresh cilantro**

¼ cup **coconut yogurt**, homemade (see page 26) or store-bought

¼ cup **Turmeric Salsa Amarillo** (page 152) or store-bought salsa

1. In a large bowl, combine the cabbage, shallots, serrano, and cilantro. Add ¼ cup of the avocado oil and 1 teaspoon of the salt and toss to coat.

2. Grease the grates with the remaining 2 tablespoons avocado oil (alternatively, in a medium grill pan, heat the oil over medium-high heat) and heat the grill to medium. Season the fish with paprika, the remaining ¼ teaspoon salt, and the garlic. When the oil is shimmering, add the fish to the grill and cook for 5 minutes per side, or until cooked through when there are grill marks on the fish.

3. Immediately assemble the tacos: Place the fish on the tortillas and top each with the spicy slaw and a squeeze of lime juice, some cilantro, coconut yogurt, and salsa, if desired.

MAPLE-GLAZED CARNITAS TACOS

Serves 12

There is a reason "low and slow" is a thing in cooking, and the phrase holds most true where meat is concerned. When you cook something this way, it allows proteins to break down, fats to render, and sugars to caramelize. You can get a wonderful depth of flavor by simply taking your time. Slow cooking is also a great method to have in your repertoire because it's so forgiving. If you forgot to set a timer and overcook by 10 minutes, everything is still juicy and delicious. Our maple-glazed carnitas are cooked this way until juicy and tender but crisp up under the broiler to get lovely crunchy edges. We love these carnitas in tacos, slathered with Turmeric Salsa Amarillo with a bit of chopped onion and cilantro.

2 tablespoons coarse **Himalayan pink salt**

½ teaspoon **ground cinnamon**

½ teaspoon **ground allspice**

2 teaspoons **ancho chili powder**

4 pounds **boneless pork shoulder**, cut into 5-inch pieces, excess fat trimmed off

¼ cup **avocado oil** or **extra-virgin olive oil**

6 cups **no-sugar-added apple juice** (preferably organic)

2 **bay leaves**

6 **garlic cloves**, smashed

1 teaspoon **ground cumin**

¼ cup **pure maple syrup**

3 tablespoons **cider vinegar**

3 recipes **Rainbow Tortillas** (page 39) or store-bought grain-free tortillas, warmed

TO GARNISH

1 cup finely diced **white onion**

1 bunch **cilantro**, coarsely chopped

2 **avocados**, sliced

Turmeric Salsa Amarillo (page 152) or store-bought salsa

1 **lime**, cut into wedges

1. Preheat the oven to 300°F.

2. In a small bowl, combine the salt, cinnamon, allspice, and chili powder. Rub the seasoning mixture all over the pork.

3. In a large Dutch oven, heat the oil over medium-high heat. When the oil is shimmering, add the pork in a single layer, working in batches as needed, and cook for about 5 minutes per side, until very well browned. Add about 1 cup water and stir, scraping up the browned bits from the bottom of the pot with a wooden spoon. Add the apple juice (and more water, if needed, to submerge the pork). Add the bay leaves, garlic, and cumin. Transfer to the oven and braise for about 4 hours, turning the pork a few times, until most of the liquid has evaporated and the pork is falling apart.

4. Transfer the pork to a large plate and shred the meat with tongs or two forks. Taste the pork and add salt as needed. Discard the liquid from the Dutch oven. Return the pork to the Dutch oven and stir in the maple syrup and vinegar. Return to the oven and cook until the pork is crispy and caramelized, about 15 minutes. For extra-crispy pork, cook for 5 minutes more under the preheated broiler.

5. To assemble the tacos, top each tortilla with pulled pork, onion, cilantro, avocado, and salsa. Serve each with a wedge of lime.

ENSENADA FRIED CAULIFLOWER TACOS

Makes 4 tacos

Growing up in Los Angeles meant trips a few hours south to Ensenada, the port on the coast of Mexico's Baja California peninsula. And trips to Ensenada always meant fish tacos—puffy, crispy, wonderful fish tacos. Inspired by these delicious textures, we created a vegetarian version with cauliflower. We love to garnish ours with our salsa verde and lots of fermented cabbage. If you want to skip the tortilla, the cauliflower and garnish are also delicious served on a bed of mixed greens with a squeeze of fresh lime juice.

¾ cup **arrowroot powder**

¼ cup **cassava flour**

1 teaspoon **baking powder,** homemade (see page 28) or store-bought

½ teaspoon **chili powder**

½ teaspoon **smoked paprika**

½ teaspoon **Himalayan pink salt**

¼ teaspoon **freshly ground black pepper**

1 **large egg,** lightly beaten

½ cup **sparkling water**

2 cups **avocado oil** or **olive oil,** for frying

¼ head **cauliflower,** cored and cut into florets (a little over 2 cups)

1 recipe **Rainbow Tortillas** (page 39) or store-bought grain-free **tortillas,** warmed

½ cup **Fermented Cabbage** (recipe follows) or store-bought (such as sauerkraut or kimchi)

1 **jalapeño pepper,** sliced

2 tablespoons **coconut yogurt,** homemade (see page 26) or store-bought

2 tablespoons **Salsa Verde,** homemade (page 151) or store-bought

1. In a large bowl, combine the arrowroot, cassava flour, baking powder, chili powder, paprika, salt, and black pepper. Stir in the egg and drizzle in the sparkling water. Mix until just combined.

2. Fill a medium heavy-bottomed skillet with avocado oil to a depth of 2 inches. Attach a deep-fry thermometer to the side and heat over medium heat until the oil reaches 375°F.

3. Working in batches, add the cauliflower to the batter, fully submerging it and letting some of the excess batter drip off, then add it to the oil, being careful not to overcrowd the pot. Fry each batch of cauliflower for about 3 minutes per side, until deeply golden brown and crisp. Place on a paper towel–lined plate to drain.

4. To assemble the tacos, top each tortilla with 3 or 4 pieces of the fried cauliflower and top with fermented cabbage, jalapeño, coconut yogurt, and salsa.

Note

We recommend using chopsticks or tongs for picking the cauliflower out of the batter and adding it to the hot oil.

FERMENTED CABBAGE

Makes 2 pints

½ head **green cabbage**, shredded

1 **carrot**, grated

½ medium **yellow onion**, thinly sliced

½ **jalapeño pepper**, thinly sliced

1 cup **cider vinegar**

3 tablespoons **fresh lime juice**

1 teaspoon **dried oregano**

1 teaspoon **freshly ground black pepper**

2 teaspoons **Himalayan pink salt**

4 cups **distilled water**

When we need to reset our gut, fermented cabbage is the place we start. Not only is it a probiotic powerhouse, which helps your gut lining better absorb nutrients, but it also tastes incredible. Perfectly zippy and bright, you can eat it solo (we do, straight out of the jar!), but it's also wonderful on top of sandwiches or even in our Ensenada-style cauliflower tacos (see opposite page).

1. In a large bowl, combine the cabbage, carrot, onion, jalapeño, vinegar, lime juice, oregano, and black pepper. Sprinkle with the salt.

2. Sterilize two pint jars. Place the jars and lids in a pot of boiling water and boil for at least 12 minutes. Drain on a paper towel and let them cool completely. Pack the vegetables into the jars. Make sure to leave about ¼ inch of headroom at the top. Add enough distilled water to completely submerge the vegetables. Cover each jar loosely with a canning lid (don't twist the lid on tightly) so it can breathe. If you have a cap with an airlock, you can use that.

3. Set the jars aside at room temperature to ferment for at least 2 days and up to 1 week, until the mixture begins to lightly bubble. Tighten the lids and store the cabbage in the refrigerator for up to 3 months.

Note

If you have glass fermentation disks to keep the cabbage under the surface of the liquid, use them to prevent mold from growing on the exposed vegetables.

ADOBO ROASTED CHICKEN TACOS

Serves 12

Adobo could mean any number of things, depending on where you are. In Mexico, it might simply mean a marinade; in Puerto Rico, it could mean a dry rub; and in the Philippines, it could mean "cooked with vinegar, spices, and coconut milk." Our inspiration for this recipe comes from the Philippines' version of adobo. The combination of vinegar and coconut milk creates a kind of buttermilk or sour milk result whereby the acid helps tenderize the chicken while adding fabulous flavor.

¼ cup **coconut aminos**

10 large **garlic cloves**, coarsely chopped

1 tablespoon **freshly ground black pepper**

1¼ cups **cider vinegar**

1 cup **whole canned tomatoes** with their liquid, coarsely chopped

2 **bay leaves**, crumbled

3 pounds boneless, skinless **chicken thighs** (about 10)

Extra-virgin olive oil or **avocado oil**, for greasing

2 medium **yellow onions**, thinly sliced

2 **scallions**, green and white parts thinly sliced

3 recipes **Rainbow Tortillas** (page 39) or store-bought grain-free **tortillas**, warmed

TO GARNISH

½ cup finely diced **onion**

1 bunch **cilantro**, coarsely chopped

2 **avocados**, sliced

Salsa Roja (page 151) or store-bought red salsa

2 **limes**, cut into wedges

1. In a large bowl, combine the coconut aminos, garlic, pepper, vinegar, tomatoes, and bay leaves. Add the chicken and submerge it in the marinade. Cover with plastic wrap and refrigerate for at least 2 hours and up to overnight.

2. Preheat the broiler. Line a rimmed baking sheet with aluminum foil and grease the foil with olive oil.

3. Transfer the chicken and marinade to a heavy-bottomed 4-quart pot. Bring the mixture to a simmer over medium heat, cover, and cook for 20 minutes, or until a meat thermometer measures 165°F internal temperature.

4. Transfer the chicken to the prepared baking sheet. Increase the heat to high and cook the marinade for about 15 minutes, until reduced by about half. Meanwhile, add the onions and scallions to the baking sheet, arranging them in an even layer with the chicken, and broil for about 5 minutes, until the chicken is crispy and browned. Let cool for about 30 minutes, then coarsely chop the chicken. Add the chicken and onions to the pot with the sauce.

5. To assemble the tacos, top each tortilla with the cooked chicken and onion, cilantro, avocado, and salsa. Serve with a lime wedge.

CARNE ASADA TACOS

Whenever we go on family vacations to Claire's mom's house in Palm Springs, a big carne asada dinner is always on the itinerary. There's a wonderful *carniceria* around the corner that has everything you need to make a Mexican feast, and we always load up on homemade salsas, guacamole, and flank steak. Carne asada is all about the marinade—it's heavy on the citrus, with some cilantro, garlic, and onion rounding out the flavors. You want a thin steak—like flank or skirt—that cooks quickly over high heat to get a juicy, crispy texture. Serve with plenty of salsa, diced onion, and cilantro, for a classic taco feast.

¼ cup **fresh lime juice**

1 cup **fresh orange juice**

4 **garlic cloves**, chopped

½ medium **yellow onion**, sliced

Leaves from 1 bunch **cilantro**, chopped

¼ cup **avocado oil**, plus more for greasing

½ teaspoon **Himalayan pink salt**

¼ teaspoon **cayenne pepper**

2 pounds **flank steak**, we prefer grass-fed

1 recipe **Rainbow Tortillas** (page 39) or store-bought grain-free **tortillas**, warmed

TO GARNISH

½ bunch **cilantro**, coarsely chopped

½ cup **dairy-free feta cheese**, homemade (see page 46) or store-bought

1 **avocado**, sliced

2 **red radishes**, thinly sliced

1. In a large bowl, combine the lime juice, orange juice, garlic, onion, cilantro, avocado oil, salt, and cayenne. Add the flank steak, cover with plastic wrap, and place in refrigerator to marinate for at least 4 hours or up to overnight.

2. Grease the grates with avocado oil and heat the grill to high and cook the steak for about 10 minutes per side, until quite firm and with dark grill marks. Transfer the steak to a cutting board and let rest for at least 10 minutes, then slice against the grain.

3. To assemble the tacos, top the tortillas with the carne asada, cilantro, cheese, avocado, and radish.

OUR FAVORITE
EGG SALAD SANDWICH

RADISH CHIVE
CHEESE SANDWICH

PESTO CHICKEN

CLASSIC CUCUMBER
SANDWICH

TEA SANDWICHES

We are eighty-five-year-old ladies at heart. We fantasize about being museum docents, love knitting, and are obsessed with afternoon tea. Claire's mum is Australian, and she grew up enjoying a "cuppa and biscuits," while Laurel's mom is a fancy lady who collects porcelain tea sets, so it only makes sense that we would bond over "putting a kettle on." A truly classic afternoon features finger sandwiches, which are meant to be light enough that they don't spoil your appetite for dinner. These are our favorites alongside a fresh pot of tea, though any of them could be enjoyed as a stand-alone sandwich as well. But when we're going all out, we like serving these open-faced to show off the fillings.

RADISH CHIVE CHEESE SANDWICH

Makes 6 sandwiches

½ cup **vegan cream cheese**, homemade (see page 44) or store-bought

1 tablespoon finely chopped **fresh chives**, plus more for garnish

½ teaspoon **freshly ground white pepper**

1 loaf **Caraway "Rye" Bread** (page 59), cut into ¼-inch slices

1 bunch **radishes**, very thinly sliced

1 teaspoon **Himalayan pink salt**

Extra-virgin olive oil, for drizzling

In a medium bowl, combine the cream cheese, chives, and white pepper. Spread the cheese mixture on each slice of bread, dividing evenly. Top each slice with enough slices of radish to cover completely, sprinkle the salt on top, and garnish with chives. Cut each slice of bread in half diagonally and cut off the crusts. Drizzle with olive oil and serve open-faced.

OUR FAVORITE EGG SALAD SANDWICH

Makes 3 sandwiches

3 large **hard-boiled eggs**

3 tablespoons **mayonnaise**, homemade (see page 29) or store-bought

1 tablespoon **cider vinegar**

Himalayan pink salt and freshly ground white pepper

½ teaspoon finely chopped **fresh dill**, plus more for garnish

3 slices **Perfect Sandwich Bread** (page 56)

1. Cut 2 of the eggs into quarters. In a high-speed blender or food processor, combine the quartered eggs, mayonnaise, vinegar, and salt and pepper and purée until just smooth and unified. Taste and add salt and pepper as needed and stir in the dill.

2. To assemble, spread a thick layer of egg salad over each slice of bread. Thinly slice the whole, remaining egg, arrange it over the egg salad, and top with dill. Cut each slice of bread in half diagonally and cut off the crusts. Serve open-faced.

CLASSIC CUCUMBER SANDWICH

Makes 8 to 10 sandwiches

1 cucumber, peeled, seeded, and sliced into ⅛-inch-thick rounds

1 tablespoon **fresh lemon juice**

1 teaspoon **Himalayan pink salt**

⅓ cup **unsalted ghee**, at room temperature, or **coconut yogurt**

1 tablespoon finely chopped **fresh mint**

1 loaf **Brioche** (page 54), cut into ¼-inch slices

½ teaspoon **freshly ground white pepper**

1. In a medium bowl, combine the cucumber slices, lemon juice, and salt. Place the cucumbers in a sieve or colander for 20 to 30 minutes to marinate and release any liquid. Transfer the cucumber slices to a paper towel–lined plate and pat dry.

2. In a small bowl, combine the ghee and mint, then spread a thin layer on one side of each slice of bread. Top half the slices with two layers of cucumber and season with white pepper. Add the remaining slices of bread on top, remove the crusts, and slice in half diagonally.

Note

To hard-boil an egg, bring a large pot of water with a splash of cider vinegar to a boil over medium-low heat. Place the eggs in the water and boil, uncovered, for 9 minutes. Drain the eggs and transfer to a large bowl of ice water to cool, for 10 to 15 minutes. Peel the eggs in the water.

PESTO CHICKEN SANDWICH

Makes 8 to 10 sandwiches

2 (4- to 5-ounce) boneless, skinless **chicken breasts**

¼ **white onion**

2 **garlic cloves**, smashed

1 **bay leaf**

5 whole **black peppercorns**

1 small handful of **fresh flat-leaf parsley**

½ cup **roasted garlic pesto** (see page 105)

2 tablespoons **mayonnaise**, homemade (see page 29) or store-bought

Himalayan pink salt and **freshly ground black pepper**

1 loaf **Perfect Sandwich Bread** (page 56)

1. Place the chicken in a large saucepan. Add the onion, garlic, bay leaf, peppercorns, and parsley and pour in enough water to cover the chicken by an inch or so. Bring to a boil over medium-high heat. Immediately reduce the heat to low, cover the pot, and let the chicken simmer for about 10 minutes, until opaque through the middle and an instant-read thermometer inserted into the thickest part reads 165°F.

2. Transfer the chicken to a plate and let cool completely, about 30 minutes. Chop the chicken into ½-inch cubes and place in a large bowl. Add the pesto and mayonnaise and stir to combine. Taste and add 1 teaspoon salt and pepper as needed.

3. Add a hearty scoop of chicken salad to a slice of bread, then top with another piece of bread, remove the crusts, and slice in half diagonally. Store any leftover chicken salad in an airtight container in the fridge for up to 5 days.

PIES, PIZZA, *and* FLATBREADS

The beauty of pies, pizza, and flatbreads is the communal activity they bring to the kitchen. It could be standing around the counter, rolling out crusts, putting toppings on a personal pizza before it goes into the oven, or tearing into a flatbread and making a meal out of dips—all of these are wonderful things to do with friends and family. These are some of our favorite recipes, and we hope you make and enjoy them with the ones you love.

SPANAKOPITA

Spanakopita is a childhood favorite of Laurel's. Growing up, she made these savory triangles with so many different family members: aunts, uncles, siblings, parents, and even close friends got in on the action. Creating the Sweet Laurel version of this dish has been a joyful way to reconnect with the tradition she holds so dear. Don't be intimidated by the process; it might seem lengthy, but it's really quite similar to any savory pie process: make the filling, make the crust, combine the two, and bake—simple as that.

FOR THE FILLING

1 tablespoon **avocado oil**

¼ cup chopped **shallot**

1 pound **fresh spinach**, chopped

3 **large eggs**

½ cup **dairy-free feta cheese**, homemade (see page 46) or store-bought

½ cup chopped **fresh dill**

¼ cup chopped **fresh mint**

½ teaspoon **Himalayan pink salt**

¼ teaspoon **cayenne pepper**

FOR THE PHYLLO DOUGH

1 cup **almond flour**

1 cup **tapioca flour**

1½ cups **full-fat canned coconut milk**

1 teaspoon **Himalayan pink salt**

2 **large eggs**, beaten with 1 tablespoon water, for egg wash

1. Preheat the oven to 350°F.

2. Make the filling. In a large skillet, heat the avocado oil over medium heat. When the oil is shimmering, add the shallot and sauté for about 3 minutes, until translucent. Add the spinach, working in batches, and cook for about 10 minutes, until bright green and wilted. Press the spinach to the side of the skillet and pour off any excess liquid. You want the spinach as dry as possible so liquid doesn't soak into the phyllo dough.

3. In a medium bowl, beat the eggs until frothy, then add the spinach mixture and stir to combine. Add the feta, dill, mint, salt, and cayenne to the bowl and stir to combine. Set aside.

4. Make the phyllo dough. Line three baking sheets with parchment paper.

5. In a large bowl, combine the almond flour, tapioca flour, coconut milk, and salt and stir until a dough forms. Measure out 2 tablespoons of the dough and, using your hands, form the dough into a ball. Place the ball on a sheet of parchment, then place another piece of parchment over the dough ball. Using a rolling pin, roll out the dough as flat and long as possible, about 8 inches long by 2 inches wide. Set the strip of dough on one of the prepared baking sheets. Repeat with the remaining dough. You should have enough dough for about 12 strips. Bake for about 3 minutes, until barely golden. The dough should be quite pale and still pliable.

6. While the dough is still warm, add about 1 tablespoon of the spinach filling to the far upper right corner of the dough. Fold the dough over the filling like a flag: Cross the far right corner of the dough across to the top of the strip, covering the filling and forming a triangle. Place the completed triangle on one of the baking sheets you used for the dough. Repeat with the remaining dough and filling.

7. Lightly brush the egg wash over the spanakopita. Bake for 12 to 15 minutes, until golden brown. Serve warm. Wrap leftover spanakopita in plastic wrap and store in the fridge for up to 5 days or in the freezer for up to 3 months. Reheat in the oven.

CHERRY TOMATO TARTE TATIN

One of Claire's favorite desserts is tarte tatin: an upside-down apple tart. It's incredibly minimalistic—butter, sugar, and apples, with a pastry base. The apples are reduced to their caramelized essence, with a pure apple flavor. We took this idea and turned it slightly savory by using cherry tomatoes instead. Roasting the tomatoes gives them a beautiful caramelized sweetness, and packing them into a pan creates a stained-glass-window effect, with the tomatoes forming a stunning geometric pattern. This tart is hearty enough to serve on its own but is also wonderful alongside scrambled eggs at a brunch or as a beautiful and impressive appetizer.

2 to 3 pints **cherry tomatoes**

4 tablespoons **olive oil**, plus more for greasing

2 **fennel bulbs**, stalks removed and bulbs sliced

3 **garlic cloves**, minced

½ teaspoon **grated nutmeg**

Himalayan pink salt and **freshly ground black pepper**

1 recipe **Savory Tart Dough** (page 34)

Arrowroot powder, for dusting

1. Preheat the oven to 425°F.

2. Place the tomatoes on a baking sheet, drizzle with 3 tablespoons of the olive oil, and toss to coat. Roast for 15 minutes, or until softened and starting to brown. Remove from the oven and set aside to cool slightly. Reduce the oven temperature to 375°F.

3. Meanwhile, in a large skillet, heat the remaining tablespoon of olive oil over medium heat. When the oil is shimmering, add the fennel and cook for 5 minutes, until the fennel is starting to brown. Add the garlic, nutmeg, and a pinch each of salt and pepper and cook for about 10 minutes more, until the fennel is tender. Remove the skillet from the heat.

4. Lightly coat a 9-inch cast-iron skillet with olive oil. Arrange the roasted cherry tomatoes in the skillet in an even layer, being careful not to overlap them.

5. Place the tart dough on a sheet of parchment paper. Lightly dust the top of the dough with arrowroot and place another sheet of parchment on top. Using a rolling pin, roll out the dough into a round about ⅛ inch thick, sprinkling with more arrowroot as needed to prevent sticking. Trim the dough so the round is a little bigger than the top of the skillet. Place the dough over the tomatoes and gently tuck the edges inside the pan.

6. Bake for about 35 minutes, until the crust is golden brown. Remove the tart from the oven and let cool to room temperature. Run a knife around the edge, then invert the tart onto a serving tray. Serve warm or at room temperature. Store leftovers, wrapped in plastic wrap, in the fridge for up to 1 week.

ZUCCHINI LATTICE TART

Serves 8 to 10

Despite her long-haired, barefoot, beachy effortlessness, Laurel is actually quite preppy. Blazers, teacups, and cashmere sweaters gently tied around her shoulders are all very much her vibe. This vibe extends into her baking, too. For every earthy, hippie-approved Coco Yo Granola Bowl (page 108), there's an afternoon-tea-ready zucchini lattice tart. The lattice topping is simple to create but always wows at gatherings. Laurel loves bringing this tart to spring picnics and serving it with a bowl of fresh strawberries.

1 teaspoon **coconut oil** or **avocado oil**, plus more for greasing

1 recipe **Savory Tart Dough** (page 34)

2 cups cooked **fresh spinach** or **frozen spinach**, thawed and drained

1 large **zucchini** (ideally 10 inches in length or longer)

3 large **eggs**

1 large **shallot**, quartered lengthwise, layers separated

1 teaspoon finely chopped **fresh tarragon leaves**

2 teaspoons chopped **fresh chives**

¼ teaspoon **cayenne pepper**

1 teaspoon **Himalayan pink salt**

Tip: For a crisp texture, at the end of the baking time, switch the oven to broil and broil for 3 minutes, until golden brown on top, then remove from the oven and let cool to the desired serving temperature.

1. Preheat the oven to 350°F. Grease a 9-inch tart pan with coconut oil.

2. Lay the tart dough on a sheet of parchment paper and place a second sheet of parchment on top. Using a rolling pin, roll out the dough to a ⅛-inch-thick, 10-inch-wide round. Press the dough into the prepared tart pan, letting the edges hang over the side of the pan a bit. Bake for 10 to 12 minutes, until golden brown. Remove the crust from the oven and set the pan on a wire rack. Trim the edges of the crust and let cool.

3. Meanwhile, in a medium skillet, melt the coconut oil over medium heat. Add the spinach and cook for 2 minutes, until bright green and wilted. Remove the skillet from the heat and drain off as much liquid as possible. Set the spinach aside.

4. Using a mandoline or a very sharp knife, thinly slice 8 long ribbons from the zucchini and set them aside, then chop the remaining zucchini to use in the filling.

5. In a medium bowl, beat the eggs until frothy. Stir in the chopped zucchini, shallot, tarragon, chives, cayenne, and salt. Add the spinach and stir to combine. Pour the mixture into the prepared crust.

6. Using the zucchini ribbons, form a lattice over the filling: Lay 4 ribbons on top of the filling, parallel to one another and with about ¾ inch of space between them. Fold back every other ribbon. Place one ribbon perpendicular to the parallel ribbons. Unfold the folded strips over the perpendicular ribbon. Now take the parallel strips that are running underneath the perpendicular strip and fold them back over the perpendicular strip, as shown to make a new row. Lay down a second perpendicular ribbon next to the first, with ¾ inch of space between them.

Unfold the folded parallel ribbons over the second ribbon. Continue this process until the lattice is complete.

7. Bake for 30 minutes, or until just set at the edges with a bit of jiggle in the center. Serve warm or at room temperature. Store, wrapped in plastic wrap, in the fridge for up to 1 week.

SCALLION PANCAKES

Sunday night Chinese food feasts cluttered with pots of tea and an always-revolving lazy Susan is just part of the culture of growing up in LA. San Gabriel Valley is home to some of the most delicious Chinese food in the country, and scallion pancakes are our favorite classic Sichuan dish. These aren't anything like fluffy American pancakes, crispy crepes, or puffy Dutch babies. They're flaky, chewy, and incredibly savory. We like them best topped with some coconut aminos and with chili oil alongside for dipping.

2 cups **arrowroot powder**

2 tablespoons **cassava flour**, plus more as needed

1 teaspoon **Himalayan pink salt**, plus more for sprinkling

1¼ cups **boiling water**, plus more as needed

1½ tablespoons **toasted sesame oil**

2 cups **scallions**, green and white parts thinly sliced

2 tablespoons **avocado oil**, for frying

Note

If you want to make the dough ahead of time, you can form the pinwheels and wrap those up individually (with plastic wrap or parchment paper) and store them in a freezer bag for up to 4 months. Thaw them in the fridge overnight and roll them out before frying. The frozen uncooked pancakes are delicate, so it is best to roll them out right before you fry them.

1. In a large bowl, whisk together the arrowroot, cassava flour, and salt. Add 1 cup of the boiling water and combine using a wooden spoon. Slowly add the remaining ¼ cup boiling water and knead well with your hands until a springy but not-sticky dough forms. If it seems dry, add up to 2 tablespoons more boiling water, being careful not to make it too wet and soft. If it gets too wet, knead in a bit more flour as necessary.

2. Divide the dough into 8 equal portions and roll them into balls with your hands. Place them in a medium bowl and cover with a damp kitchen towel. Lay one portion of dough on a sheet of parchment paper and cover with another sheet. Using a rolling pin, roll the dough into a circle, about ⅛ inch thick. Remove the parchment and brush on a thin layer of toasted sesame oil on the top of the dough.

3. Add ¼ cup of the minced scallions to the flattened dough and sprinkle with salt. Carefully roll the dough into an even cylinder, like a cigar, then coil the dough into a pinwheel shape. Place the pinwheel between the two pieces of parchment paper and flatten it into a thin circular pancake, about 5 inches wide and ⅛ inch thick with a tortilla press or a rolling pin. Repeat with the remaining dough balls.

4. Heat a large skillet over medium heat. Add the avocado oil. Once the oil is shimmering, place one pancake at a time in the skillet and cook for 5 minutes, or until browned. Brush some hot oil on the side facing you, then flip and fry for 3 minutes more, or until crispy and browned. Remove the pancake from the skillet and set on a rack to cool slightly. Repeat with the remaining dough. Serve warm.

ROTI

Makes 10 rotis

Making traditional roti is quite a process—you slap the dough against a counter, stretching it until the dough is windowpane thin and basically held together with a whispered prayer. This isn't the case with our recipe for a simple reason: there's no gluten. Stretching and resting is a huge part of preparing traditional, wheat-based goods. The gluten creates structure, and the rhythm of stretching and resting (like kneading) gives the dough that pliability. In our recipe, we get stretch and chewiness from arrowroot, and the boiling water helps give it more of a glutinous stretch. Crispy, chewy, golden brown—these delicious little flatbreads are the perfect counterpoint to spicy Thai-style curry, but on the streets of Thailand, you can find stands that top them with sweet or savory garnishes, just like a crepe. They're a delight with any dish!

⅔ cup **cassava flour**

⅓ cup **arrowroot powder**

¼ teaspoon **Himalayan pink salt**

1 tablespoon **extra-virgin olive oil**, plus more for greasing

1 cup **hot water** (110° to 130°F)

1. In a large bowl, combine the cassava flour, arrowroot, salt, and olive oil. Using a rubber spatula, stir in the hot water. When the mixture is cool enough to be handled but still warm, use your hands to knead the dough and make a smooth dough ball. Divide the dough into 10 equal portions and roll each into a ball. Using a rolling pin, roll each ball into a 4-inch round.

2. Heat a large skillet over medium heat and lightly grease with olive oil. Place one round in the pan and cook until it bubbles and puffs slightly, about 1 minute, then flip and cook for 1 minute more. There should be irregular dark brown spots. Remove the roti from the skillet and let cool before serving.

3. Repeat with the remaining rounds, greasing the pan each time, or store them in an air-tight container in the refrigerator for up to 2 days.

GARLIC NAAN

Before his semester abroad in India, Claire's husband, Craig, ate like a toddler: chicken fingers, ketchup on the side, white and brown food only, and definitely no spice. But ten weeks of eating chana masala, samosas, and every kind of curry changed his palette entirely. When he returned home, his plate became a riot of color and spice—no pepper was too hot. But Craig shifted his diet to paleo, and one of the things he missed most was naan. No Indian feast is complete without a giant pile of this puffy, blistered flatbread. That's because naan is not for the sidelines: naan can be the cutlery, the plate, and/or the meal itself. This naan is particularly lovely if you serve it with some extra melted ghee for dipping.

2¼ teaspoons **active dry yeast**

1 cup **warm water** (100° to 110°F)

¼ cup **pure maple syrup**

1 **large egg**, beaten

1 teaspoon **Himalayan pink salt**

1¾ cups **cassava flour**, plus more for dusting

1¼ cups **almond flour**

1 cup **arrowroot powder**

¼ cup **minced garlic**

Unsalted ghee, melted, for garnish

½ cup chopped **flat-leaf parsley** or cilantro

1. In a large bowl, dissolve the yeast in the warm water. Let sit in a warm area—in direct sunlight, for instance (about 80°F is ideal)—until foaming and bubbling, 5 to 10 minutes. Stir in the maple syrup, egg, salt, both flours, and arrowroot until a soft dough forms. Place the dough in a bowl, cover with a damp kitchen towel, and let sit until the dough has risen by 30 percent.

2. Using your hands, shape the dough into a long rectangle and cut into 12 equal portions, dusting with more cassava flour as necessary.

3. Preheat the oven to 200°F, to keep naan warm between batches.

4. Lay one portion of dough on a sheet of parchment paper, sprinkle with a teaspoon of garlic, and cover with another sheet of parchment. Using a rolling pin, roll the dough into an oval shape about ¼ inch thick. Place the skillet over medium-high heat. Remove the top layer of parchment and, placing your hand under the bottom layer of parchment, flip the dough onto the skillet, remove the parchment, and cook until the bottom is golden and blackened in spots, about 4 minutes. Flip the naan and cook for 2 to 3 minutes more, until lightly browned and blistered. Remove the naan from the pan, brush with ghee, sprinkle with parsley or cilantro, and serve warm. Repeat with the remaining portions of dough, reducing the heat if the pan becomes too hot.

5. Place the cooked naan on a baking sheet in the oven to keep warm until ready to serve. To store, wrap the naan in plastic and keep in the fridge for up to 2 weeks or in the freezer for up to 3 months. Reheat in the oven.

SPINACH ARTICHOKE FLATBREAD

When we were in high school, a "big night out" meant being dropped off at the corner of the Westwood Village. There were two movie theaters, an excellent bakery with 25-cent cookies, and a California Pizza Kitchen, or "CPK" to the cool kids, which we definitely were not. You ordered two things there: BBQ chicken pizza and the spinach artichoke dip. We felt exceedingly adult ordering an appetizer, especially one that felt so elegant to our fifteen-year-old selves. Here we have turned the dish into a grown-up flatbread, basically the dip and the bread baked together. Our version, of course, omits the dairy, but it does not lack in flavor. For a big party, we like to slice the flatbread into easy-to-grab strips, about 2 inches wide, with a squeeze of lemon and flaky salt on top. Served whole, the flatbread is wonderful alongside a soup or salad, or on its own as a snack.

1 cup **vegan cream cheese**, homemade (see page 44) or store-bought

¼ teaspoon **Himalayan pink salt**

½ teaspoon **freshly ground black pepper**

½ teaspoon **garlic powder**

Pinch of **cayenne pepper**

1 cup thawed, chopped **frozen spinach**, squeezed and drained

1½ cups thawed, chopped **frozen artichoke hearts**

1 recipe **Garlic Naan** (page 223), uncooked

Note

To store, wrap the flatbread in plastic and keep in the fridge for up to 2 weeks or in the freezer for up to 3 months. Reheat in the oven.

1. Preheat the oven to 200°F.

2. In a small bowl, combine the cream cheese, salt, black pepper, garlic powder, and cayenne and mix until smooth, then fold in the spinach and artichokes.

3. Heat a large cast-iron or heavy-bottom skillet over medium-high heat until very hot.

4. Using your hands, roll 3 tablespoons of dough into a ball, then press a divot into the center. Fill the divot with 1½ tablespoons of the cream cheese mixture, add another 2 tablespoons of dough on top of the filling, and gently press the dough together to bind. Lay the stuffed dough on a sheet of parchment paper and cover with another sheet. Using a rolling pin, roll the dough into an oval shape about ¼ inch thick and 6 inches long.

5. Remove the top layer of parchment, flip the stuffed flatbread onto the dry skillet, and peel away the second layer of parchment. Cook for 2 to 3 minutes, until the bottom is golden and blackened in spots, flip, then cook for 2 minutes more, until the bottom is lightly browned and blistered in spots. Remove the flatbread from the skillet. Place the flatbread on a baking sheet in the oven to keep warm until serving. Repeat with remaining ingredients for the last 9 flatbreads.

SESAME SPECKLED TAHINI FLATBREAD

If Claire were to choose just one favorite meal, it would be bread and butter. Excellent bread with excellent butter. The act of tearing bread, spreading or dipping it, and devouring it, bite by bite—that's luxurious. You're taking the time to savor and enjoy. This flatbread is a wonderful bread to savor—and it's built for dipping. The crunchy, chewy texture is an enticing contrast against creamy dips or even a simple, grassy olive oil. It also works deliciously as a sandwich bread with shredded chicken, crisp cucumbers, and mayo (see page 29), or you could load it up with avocado, greens, and our tzatziki sauce (see page 147).

⅔ cup **warm water** (100° to 110°F)

1 tablespoon **honey**

2 heaping tablespoons **active dry yeast**

2 tablespoons **sesame seeds**

2 teaspoons **ground coriander**

2 teaspoons **ground cumin**

2 teaspoons **dried thyme**

2½ cups **almond flour**

¼ cup **arrowroot powder**

¼ cup **tapioca starch**

1 tablespoon **extra-virgin olive oil,** plus more for greasing and drizzling

¼ cup **tahini**

3 large **egg whites**

3 **garlic cloves**, minced

½ teaspoon **sea salt**

1 teaspoon **cider vinegar**

1. Place the warm water, honey, and yeast in a small bowl, stir once, and let it sit in a warm place—in direct sunlight, for instance (about 80°F is ideal)—until foaming and bubbling, about 5 minutes. In a separate small bowl, combine the sesame seeds, coriander, cumin, and thyme.

2. In the bowl of a stand mixer fitted with the paddle attachment, combine the almond flour, arrowroot, tapioca starch, and 1 tablespoon of the spice mixture and beat on medium until fully incorporated. Add the oil, tahini, egg whites, garlic, and salt and continue beating until smooth. Add the vinegar and yeast mixture and beat for 2 minutes more, or until a soft and sticky dough forms. Cover the bowl with plastic wrap and let the dough rise for about 2 hours, until puffy but not quite doubled in size.

3. Preheat the oven to 375°F. Grease a baking sheet with olive oil and line with parchment paper.

4. Using a wet spatula, spread the dough onto the prepared pan. Drizzle with oil and top with the remaining spice mixture. Bake for about 30 minutes, until the bread is golden brown. Remove from the oven, set on a rack, and let cool for 15 minutes before serving.

SICILIAN PAN PIZZA

Unlike a Neapolitan pizza—round, chewy, and puffy at the edges—Sicilian pizza is square, crispy, and almost caramelized. It's incredibly good, and a completely different pizza experience. This is what you tell yourself in the second hour of your wait outside of Prince St. Pizza in New York's SoHo neighborhood. Prince St. Pizza makes, in our opinion, the most perfect iteration of Sicilian crust pizza outside of Sicily. The key is the marvelously dark crust, which walks that tightrope between burnt and deeply caramelized. To replicate it at home, we love that you can just press the dough into the pan and let it crisp up to perfection. We're not sure why, but something about this style of pizza demands hearty, even spicy, toppings. We serve this with our Caesar Salad (page 172) for a classic Friday night at home in our favorite sweats.

2 tablespoons **extra-virgin olive oil**, plus more for greasing and drizzling

4 teaspoons **active dry yeast**

4 teaspoons **maple syrup** or **honey**

½ cup **warm water** (100° to 110°F)

3½ cups **almond flour**

2 cups **arrowroot powder**

1 tablespoon **baking powder**, homemade (see page 28) or store-bought

Himalayan pink salt

2 large **eggs**, at room temperature

6 large **egg whites**, at room temperature

4 teaspoons **cider vinegar**

¾ cup **Sicilian Tomato Sauce** (recipe follows)

½ cup **fresh basil leaves**, chiffonade

1. Preheat the oven to 450°F. Line two baking sheets with parchment and grease with olive oil.

2. In a large bowl, combine the yeast, maple syrup, and warm water. Cover with a damp kitchen towel and let sit in a warm area—in direct sunlight, for instance (about 80°F is ideal)—until foaming and bubbling, 5 to 10 minutes.

3. In a medium bowl, whisk together the almond flour, arrowroot, baking powder, and 1 teaspoon salt until fully combined.

4. Add the egg, egg whites, oil, and vinegar to the bowl with the yeast. Using a whisk or a handheld mixer on low, whisk for 2 to 3 minutes, until light and frothy. Add the flour mixture in two batches and mix until a soft dough forms. Cover with a damp kitchen towel and let the dough rise for 1 to 2 hours, until it has expanded by about 30 percent.

5. Tip the dough out onto a piece of parchment and cut in half. Put 1 piece of dough on each baking sheet, pressing down to spread it across, until about ½ inch thick. Cover each dough with half of the tomato sauce, leaving 1 inch of dough exposed at the edge. Bake for 15 to 20 minutes, until the crust is deep golden brown.

6. To serve, drizzle each with oil and sprinkle with fresh basil and salt.

recipe continues

SICILIAN TOMATO SAUCE

Makes 3 cups

2 tablespoons **extra-virgin olive oil**

3 **garlic cloves**, minced

½ teaspoon **Himalayan pink salt**

2 teaspoons **freshly ground black pepper**

1 (24-ounce) can **crushed tomatoes**

3 ounces **tomato paste**

2 teaspoons **fresh rosemary**, chopped

2 teaspoons **fresh basil**, chopped

1 whole **clove**

Pinch of **red pepper flakes**

½ teaspoon **pure maple syrup**

1. Heat the olive oil in a medium saucepan over medium heat. When the oil is shimmering, add the garlic and toast very lightly, about 30 seconds. Reduce the heat to low and add the salt, black pepper, tomatoes, tomato paste, rosemary, basil, clove, red pepper flakes, maple syrup, and 1 cup water. Cover and simmer for about 1 hour, until bubbling and thickened. Remove the clove and, if desired, blend the sauce in a high-speed blender until smooth, about 1 minute.

2. Store in an airtight container in the fridge for up to 1 week or freeze for up to 3 months.

PIZZA SPREAD

When one of the top pizza restaurants in LA, Pizzana, launched a gluten-free crust, Laurel was practically hovering next to the wood-burning oven as the first pie came out. Laurel loves pizza, especially Nea-California style, a hybrid of Neapolitan pizza and California farmers' market flavors. When we developed our grain-free crust, Laurel turned out batch after batch of delicious pizza—the recipes here are her three favorites. Two of the recipes call for our homemade cheeses, which we suggest making the day before if you have the time. Laurel can also tolerate buffalo milk, which is lactose-free, so if you want to replace the homemade dairy-free cheese with bufala mozzarella, go for it.

CLASSIC MARGHERITA PIZZA
Makes one 10-inch pizza

Pizza Dough (page 35)
¼ cup **Sicilian Tomato Sauce** (page 228)
1 cup 1½-inch cubes **Dairy-Free Mozzarella** (page 47)
Fresh basil, for garnish

1. Preheat the oven to 500°F. If you have a pizza stone, place it directly on the oven rack while it preheats. If not, place an inverted baking sheet on the oven rack while the oven preheats. The baking sheet will get very hot and provide a crispy bottom crust.

2. On a counter, place the dough on a sheet of parchment, cover with another piece of parchment paper, and gently roll out into a large circle, about 10 inches in diameter and ⅛ inch thick. Using your fingers, pinch the edge of the pizza dough into a small lip. Spread the sauce over the pizza dough, but not the lip, and sprinkle with the mozzarella and fresh basil. Bake for 12 to 15 minutes, until the dough is deep golden brown at the edges.

OUR FAVORITE BIANCA

Makes one 10-inch pizza

Pizza Dough (page 35)

2 tablespoons extra-virgin olive oil

1 cup sliced **Dairy-Free Mozzarella** (page 47)

½ cup crumbled **Dairy-Free Parmesan** (page 46)

½ cup **Classic Vegan Cream Cheese** (page 44), spooned into small balls

Freshly ground black pepper

1. Preheat the oven to 500°F. If you have a pizza stone, place it directly on the oven rack while it preheats. If not, place an inverted baking sheet on the oven rack while the oven preheats. The baking sheet will get very hot and provide a crispy bottom crust.

2. On a counter, place the dough on a sheet of parchment paper, cover with another piece of parchment paper, and gently roll out into a large circle, about 10 inches in diameter and ⅛ inch thick. Using your fingers, pinch the edge of the pizza dough into a small lip. Spread olive oil evenly over the pizza dough, but not the lip, and sprinkle with the mozzarella, parmesan, cream cheese, and pepper. Bake for 15 minutes, or until golden brown at the edges.

SUMMER VEGETABLE PIZZA

Makes one 10-inch pizza

Pizza Dough (page 35)

¼ cup **Sicilian Tomato Sauce** (page 228)

½ medium **zucchini**, thinly sliced

¼ **red onion**, thinly sliced

¼ cup pitted **black olives**, halved

1 **bell pepper**, seeded and cored, diced

Pinch of **Himalayan pink salt**

2 tablespoons extra-virgin olive oil

1. Preheat the oven to 500°F. If you have a pizza stone, place it directly on the oven rack while it preheats. If not, place an inverted baking sheet on the oven rack while the oven preheats. The baking sheet will get very hot and provide a crispy bottom crust.

2. On a counter, place the dough on a sheet of parchment paper, cover with another piece of parchment paper, and gently roll out into a large circle, about 10 inches in diameter and ⅛ inch thick. Using your fingers, pinch the edge of the pizza dough into a small lip. Spoon the sauce over the pizza dough, sprinkle with zucchini, onion, olives, pepper, and salt, then drizzle with olive oil, but not the lip, and sprinkle more salt, if desired. Bake for 15 minutes, or until the crust is deep golden brown at the edges.

FEAST

If we know one thing for sure, it's that feasting is much more of an emotional state than an actual event. Our hosting isn't usually a fussy affair but rather a casual and relaxed moment with the people we care for. But even a meal eaten on the couch with a loved one or shared at a kitchen counter with a confidant over conversation can still be special. For us, the shift from a meal to a feast is the feeling of abundance and sumptuousness. The flavors and textures are thoughtful and delicious; you enjoy each bite with intention. Feasting is a love language that can provide nourishment of every sort. Eat with your heart open, ready to receive joy from each bite.

AUSSIE MEAT PIE

Serves 8 to 10

Aussie meat pie has been called "Australia's national dish." On Claire's numerous trips Down Under to visit her family, she'd always stop into a tuck shop (a corner bakery) and pick up a few. Traditionally, they're mini pies filled with lamb and dolloped with tomato sauce (ketchup), but this version with grass-fed beef and plenty of vegetables is large enough for a big family meal. The trick is to brown the meat and cook the vegetables before assembling to prevent the pie from getting soupy, while staying perfectly moist and rich.

2 tablespoons **unsalted ghee** or **extra-virgin olive oil**

1 cup chopped **yellow onion**

4 **garlic cloves**, minced

1 cup diced **carrots**

1 cup chopped **shiitake mushrooms**

½ cup diced **turnips**

½ cup diced **celery stalk**

1½ pounds **ground lamb or beef**, 85% lean

2 tablespoons **arrowroot powder**, plus more for dusting

1 teaspoon **Himalayan pink salt**

1 teaspoon **freshly ground black pepper**

1 tablespoon **tomato paste**

½ cup **beef broth**

1 tablespoon **cider vinegar**

½ teaspoon **ground mustard**

½ teaspoon **onion powder**

1 teaspoon **garlic powder**

1 teaspoon chopped **fresh rosemary** leaves

1 teaspoon chopped **fresh thyme** leaves

1 teaspoon chopped **fresh sage**

1 tablespoon finely chopped **fresh flat-leaf parsley**

1 **Savory Tart Dough** (page 34)

1 **large egg**, beaten with 1 teaspoon water, for egg wash

1. Preheat the oven to 375°F. Line a baking sheet with parchment paper.

2. Melt the ghee in a large skillet over medium-high heat. Add the onion and sauté until it begins to take on color, 10 to 15 minutes. Stir in the garlic, carrots, mushrooms, turnips, and celery and cook for another 10 minutes, until the mushrooms have let out their liquid. Add the lamb, arrowroot, salt, and pepper and stir to combine. Cook until the lamb has browned all over, about 5 minutes. Stir in the tomato paste, broth, vinegar, ground mustard, onion powder, garlic powder, rosemary, thyme, sage, and parsley and stir to combine. Once the mixture is at a boil, immediately reduce the heat to low, cover, and simmer for 10 minutes, or until the sauce is thickened slightly.

3. On a counter, lay out a piece of parchment paper, lightly dust with arrowroot, and place the dough on top. Lightly dust the top of the dough with arrowroot and place another sheet of parchment paper on top. Using a rolling pin, roll out the dough into a large circle, about 12 inches in diameter and ⅛ inch thick. Continue sprinkling with arrowroot to ensure the dough doesn't stick to the paper.

4. Pour the lamb mixture into an 9-inch pie dish, spreading it with a spatula. Carefully cover the mixture with the dough, pressing it around the edges to create a seal. Slice in four air vents on top. Repair any cracks with a wet finger. Brush the dough with the egg wash.

5. Place the pie dish on the prepared baking sheet and bake for 40 to 45 minutes, until golden brown on top. Remove the pie from the oven, set on a rack, and let cool for 15 minutes before serving.

LAUREL'S MOUSSAKA

Serves 4 to 6

Some families have mom's meat loaf; Laurel grew up with mom's moussaka. Moussaka is traditionally made with layers of potatoes, eggplant, lamb, and béchamel sauce, so when Laurel shifted her diet but craved something nostalgic, she started playing around with this dish. Our version removes the potatoes and the béchamel sauce, making it lighter but still a perfect meal for a cozy night in or a celebratory evening with family. The addition of a bit of cinnamon pairs nicely with the gamey flavor of lamb. This is the perfect dish to make for a crowd and can easily be doubled if your family is as large as Laurel's.

2 medium **eggplants**

2 teaspoons **Himalayan pink salt**

1 pound **ground lamb**, 85% to 90% lean

1 medium **yellow onion**, chopped

4 **garlic cloves**, chopped

1 (12.5-ounce) can **fire-roasted tomatoes**, drained

½ teaspoon **ground cinnamon**

½ cup chopped **fresh dill**

2 tablespoons **avocado oil**, plus more for greasing

1 quart **coconut** or **sheep's milk yogurt**

2 large **eggs**

1. Preheat the oven to 400°F.

2. Peel the eggplants, cut into ½-inch-thick rounds, place in a colander, and sprinkle with 1 teaspoon of the salt. Let the eggplants sweat for about 20 minutes. To make sure the moussaka isn't soggy, we want the eggplant to release some of its liquid before cooking with it.

3. Heat a large skillet over medium heat. Add the lamb and cook until browned, about 10 minutes. Transfer the lamb to a medium bowl and set aside. Pour off all but 1 tablespoon fat from the skillet.

4. Return the skillet to medium heat. Add the onion and garlic and sauté, stirring occasionally, for 15 minutes, until lightly golden. Add the tomatoes, the remaining teaspoon of salt, the cinnamon, and the dill. Increase the heat to medium-high and simmer for about 20 minutes, until a lightly thickened sauce forms. Stir in the ground lamb and any collected juices from the plate and cook for 10 minutes more until slightly reduced and thickened.

5. Meanwhile, heat the avocado oil in a separate large skillet over medium heat. When the oil is shimmering, add the eggplant and sauté for about 7 minutes per side, until golden brown. Layer the cooked eggplant into the bottom of a greased 9 × 13-inch casserole dish, overlapping slightly and covering the pan, and pour the lamb mixture over the eggplant, smoothing out the top with a spatula.

6. In small bowl, beat together the yogurt and eggs until smooth. Pour the yogurt mixture over the moussaka. Bake for 45 minutes, until bubbling with golden brown spots, and allow to cool slightly before serving.

CLASSIC CHICKEN POTPIE

Serves 5 to 7

Does it get any cozier than a chicken potpie? On rainy school days, which isn't very often in LA, Claire's mom would let her stay home, get manicures, and make a big chicken potpie. A flaky, golden brown crust covering its perfectly creamy filling is exactly the thing to enjoy on a cold evening. But how do you achieve creaminess without cream? For us, the secret is in cashews. When soaked and blended, cashews take on a wonderfully silky texture. Cashew cream is one of our favorite "secret ingredients" to add a velvety texture to anything. And to keep this dish super simple, we use rotisserie chicken.

5 tablespoons unsalted ghee

1 cup chopped carrot

1 cup chopped celery

½ cup thinly sliced leeks

½ cup diced yellow onion

1 teaspoon chopped fresh thyme

2 teaspoons chopped fresh tarragon

¼ cup arrowroot powder, plus more for dusting

1 tablespoon coconut butter

2 cups chicken broth, plus more as needed

1 cup cashew cream or coconut cream

½ teaspoon grated nutmeg

1½ teaspoons Himalayan pink salt

¼ teaspoon freshly ground black pepper

3 cups ½-inch pieces rotisserie chicken breast

1½ cups chopped asparagus

1 recipe Rough Puff Pastry (page 33), thawed

1 large egg, beaten with 1 teaspoon water, for egg wash

1. Preheat the oven to 375°F.

2. Melt 2 tablespoons of the ghee in a large skillet over medium-high heat. Add the carrot, celery, leeks, onion, thyme, and tarragon and cook, stirring frequently, until slightly softened but not browned, about 5 minutes. Transfer the vegetables to a large bowl.

3. Wipe out the skillet and return it to medium heat. Melt the remaining 3 tablespoons ghee, then add the arrowroot and coconut butter and cook, whisking continuously, until the mixture bubbles and is fragrant, about 5 minutes. Whisk in the broth and cook, whisking continuously, about 1 minute until velvety smooth. Whisk in the cashew cream and cook for 2 to 3 minutes more, until just thickened. Stir in the nutmeg, salt, and pepper. If the sauce is too thick, whisk in more broth as needed.

4. Add the chicken, asparagus, and sauce to the vegetables and stir until fully incorporated. Pour the mixture into a 9 × 13 baking dish.

5. On a counter, lay out a piece of parchment paper, lightly dust with arrowroot, and place the dough on top. Lightly dust the top of the dough with arrowroot and place another sheet of parchment paper on top. Using a rolling pin, roll out the dough to at least 11 × 15 inches, to cover the entire dish. Flip the dough from the parchment paper onto the baking dish. Fold the edges over the sides and crimp to seal. Using the tip of a knife, create three small vent holes near the center of the potpie. Lightly brush the crust with the egg wash.

6. Set the baking dish on a baking sheet and place in the middle rack in the oven. Bake for 40 to 50 minutes, until the pastry is golden brown and crisp. Then turn the oven to broil and broil for 3 to 4 minutes to brown the crust, if needed. Let cool for 10 minutes before serving.

WHOLE ROASTED CHICKEN *with* CROUTONS

Cher Horowitz, the patron saint of teenage LA girls, gives the advice that "whenever a boy comes over, always have something baking." We'd like to suggest roasting a chicken as an option as well. The aromas that waft out of your oven will drive any person with an appetite wild with hunger. A roast chicken can be a cozy evening with your family, an afternoon picnic with friends, or a few nights of dinner for yourself—it's incredibly versatile and as elegant as it is familiar and comforting. The only thing that could improve a perfectly roasted chicken is an abundance of crusty croutons to soak up all of those delicious juices. Serve with a jar of Dijon mustard (seriously—it's so good with these flavors) and enjoy!

1 (3-pound) **whole chicken**, rinsed and patted dry

2 teaspoons **Himalayan pink salt**, plus more to taste

2 teaspoons **freshly ground white pepper**

3 tablespoons **Dijon mustard**, homemade (see page 28) or store-bought

3 tablespoons **extra-virgin olive oil**, plus more for drizzling

1 **Perfect Sandwich Bread** (page 56), or store-bought loaf, cut into 1-inch cubes

1 teaspoon **fresh thyme** leaves, plus more for garnish

Freshly ground black pepper

1. Preheat the oven to 425°F.

2. Remove the giblets from the chicken and discard them. Place the chicken, breast side down, on a 2-foot-long horizontal piece of kitchen twine, so the chicken's back is facing you. Tuck the wings behind the chicken's back with your hands. Cross the twine underneath the front tip of the breast bone, pulling to tighten. Crisscross the ends of the legs and use the remainder of string to tie them together in a knot. Rub the chicken all over with the salt, white pepper, mustard, and olive oil. Place the cubes of bread on a roasting pan and drizzle with enough oil to lightly coat each cube. Add the thyme and black pepper and more salt if desired, then toss to coat.

3. Roast the chicken for 50 minutes. At this point the chicken will be starting to brown. Remove from the oven and baste the chicken with the pan juices. Return to the oven and roast until a thermometer inserted into the upper thigh reads 165°F, 30 to 35 minutes more. Remove the chicken from the oven and place on a carving board, cover with aluminum foil, and let the chicken rest for 10 minutes before carving.

4. Meanwhile, toss the bread cubes in the juices and return to the oven, cooking for another 10 to 15 minutes, until golden brown and toasted. Remove from the oven and place on a large platter.

5. To serve, place the chicken on a bed of croutons, drizzle with au jus, and garnish with thyme.

SWEET POTATO CURRY

When you think of food in Los Angeles, tacos, sushi, and juice cleanses probably all come to mind. Those are important threads in our cultural fabric as a city, but there are so many others, too. In this dish, we celebrate Thai Town, the neighborhood in East Hollywood filled with incredible Thai restaurants and culture. This bright, savory, spicy panaang is a wonderful "intro to curry" dish for people who haven't experienced Thai food before—the coconut milk gives it a velvety texture that mellows out the spice. At Sweet Laurel, we don't have soy sauce or fish sauce in our pantry. To get the same umami savory flavor profile, we use anchovies (which melt into the sauce) and coconut aminos. This dish is wonderful with sweet potatoes but also with chunks of hanger steak.

½ teaspoon **ground coriander**

½ teaspoon **ground cumin**

1 teaspoon **lime zest**

2½ tablespoons **All-Purpose Curry Paste** (recipe follows)

1 tablespoon **avocado** or **olive oil**

1 **anchovy**

1 (13.5-ounce) can **full-fat canned coconut milk**

1 teaspoon **Himalayan pink salt**

1 tablespoon **coconut aminos**

1 teaspoon **honey**

1 pound **sweet potatoes**, peeled and cut into 1½-inch pieces

1 tablespoon **cashew** or **almond butter**

1 **Fresno chile**, seeded and cut into thin slivers, for garnish

Makrut lime leaves (see Note), for garnish

1. Heat a medium skillet over low heat. Add the coriander and cumin and toast, stirring occasionally, for about 1 minute, until fragrant. Transfer the toasted spices to a small bowl. Add the lime zest and curry paste and stir until fully incorporated.

2. Heat the avocado oil in a medium saucepan over medium heat and add the anchovy. When the oil is shimmering, add the coconut milk and salt and cook, stirring occasionally, until the mixture begins to bubble. Reserve 1 tablespoon of the milk in a small bowl, then stir in the curry paste mixture, coconut aminos, honey, and 1 cup water. Add the sweet potatoes and reduce the heat to medium, cover, and cook, stirring occasionally, until the sweet potatoes are tender, about 25 minutes. Let simmer 10 minutes more to thicken, until the consistency resembles a light gravy. Stir in the nut butter and immediately remove from heat.

3. Divide the curry among bowls and garnish with a splash of the reserved coconut milk, the sliced chile, and lime leaves. Serve with a side of roti, either homemade (see page 220) or store-bought.

Note

If you can't find makrut (also called kaffir) lime leaves, use Thai basil.

ALL-PURPOSE CURRY PASTE

Makes 1 cup

½ cup thinly sliced **lemongrass**

Himalayan pink salt

¼ cup coarsely sliced **ginger**

10 large **dried ancho chiles**, stemmed and seeded

4 **makrut lime leaves**, deveined and julienned (see Note, page 244)

½ cup coarsely sliced **shallots**

¾ cup **garlic cloves**

⅓ cup **avocado oil** or **olive oil**

1. In a food processor or blender, pulse the lemongrass with a pinch of salt until finely chopped. Add the ginger, another pinch of salt, and pulse again until combined, scraping down the sides with a spatula as needed. Repeat with the chiles, lime leaves, shallots, and garlic cloves, one by one, until fully incorporated and a thick semi-dry paste forms.

2. Heat the avocado oil in a small skillet over medium-low heat. When the oil is shimmering, stir in the curry paste and cook until the oil is combined and the mixture is very fragrant, 5 to 10 minutes. Let cool completely, for about 20 minutes, then transfer to an airtight container and store in the fridge for up to 3 weeks, or in the freezer for up to 3 months.

BREAD CRUMB–COATED CHICKEN

We love creating contrast on our plate, and crispy, golden chicken cutlets over a plate of vegetables is one of our favorites. This chicken is not unlike schnitzel, hammered thin and coated in bread crumbs before being sautéed until bronzed perfection, then baked through. This is also a good recipe to have on hand for days-old bread you can't bear to throw out. We love pairing it with the Caramelized Lemon Broccoli Salad (page 143).

FOR THE CHICKEN

2 boneless, skinless **chicken breasts**, butterflied and halved (4 pieces total)

Himalayan pink salt and **freshly ground white pepper**

¾ cup **cassava flour**

¼ cup **arrowroot powder**

2 **large eggs**

2 tablespoons **full-fat canned coconut milk**

2 cups unseasoned **grain-free bread crumbs**, homemade (see page 34) or store-bought

Coconut oil or **olive oil**, for frying

Lemon wedges, for garnish

1. Preheat the oven to 350°F. Line a baking sheet with parchment paper.

2. Working with one piece at a time, place the chicken in a large zip-top bag, or between two pieces of plastic wrap or wax paper, and pound until ¼ inch thin. Place the chicken on a large platter and season lightly on both sides with salt and pepper.

3. In a medium shallow bowl, combine the cassava flour and arrowroot. In a separate medium shallow bowl, whisk together the eggs and coconut milk. Place the bread crumbs in a third medium shallow bowl.

4. Fill a large, deep cast-iron skillet with coconut oil to a depth of 1 inch. Attach a deep-fry thermometer to the side and heat the oil over medium heat to 350°F.

5. Meanwhile, again working with one piece at a time, dredge the chicken in the flour mixture, shaking off any excess, then dip them in the egg mixture, allowing any excess to drip off, and finally dredge in the bread crumbs, pressing to coat. Set the chicken on a wire rack while you coat the remaining pieces.

6. Working in batches, add the chicken to the oil and fry for about 1 minute, gently moving the skillet in circular motion on the burner, until the coating looks bubbly and starts to brown, then turn and cook for 1 minute more, or until chicken registers 165°F with meat thermometer. Transfer the fried chicken to paper towel–lined plate to drain and repeat with the remaining chicken, letting the oil return to temperature between batches.

7. Place the chicken on the prepared baking sheet, and bake until cooked through and golden brown, 10 to 15 minutes.

8. Serve the chicken with Caramelized Lemon Broccoli Salad (page 143) and garnish with lemon wedges.

WHOLE ROASTED CAULIFLOWER *with*
AVOCADO HUMMUS AND GREMOLATA BREAD CRUMBS

Cauliflower enjoys an entirely different identity when it's roasted. Its starchy elements become caramelized, almost like candy, and it takes on other flavors beautifully. This simple recipe is a perfect vegan main course—the whole cauliflower almost looks like a Thanksgiving turkey it's so dynamic, and the crispy but tender cauliflower with the creamy avocado hummus creates a delicious contrast. Add a dairy-free cheese (see pages 46 to 47) on top for a decadent finishing touch.

1 large head of **cauliflower**

¼ cup **olive oil**, for roasting

Himalayan pink salt

2 cups **Fresh Avocado Hummus**
 (page 146)

¼ cup **Gremolata Bread Crumbs**
 (recipe follows)

1. Place a large ovenproof skillet in the oven and place a small saucepan of water on the floor of the oven. Preheat the oven to 375°F.

2. Remove the bottom of the stem and the leaves from the cauliflower, then cut out the core of the cauliflower, being careful not to cut any of the florets. Rinse the cauliflower, drizzle olive oil and rub all over, then sprinkle with salt. Remove the skillet from the oven and place the cauliflower on it. Cook, basting occasionally with oil, until fork-tender all the way through and golden brown, 1 to 2 hours. Turn the oven to broil and cook for 5 minutes more, until the top is crisp and brown.

3. Serve the whole cauliflower over avocado hummus and top with the Gremolata Bread Crumbs. Cut the cauliflower into wedges to enjoy.

GREMOLATA BREAD CRUMBS
Makes 1 cup

1 cup **grain-free bread crumbs**,
 homemade (see page 34) or other
 bread crumbs

2 teaspoons finely chopped **fresh flat-leaf
 parsley**

3 **garlic cloves**, minced

1 tablespoon **lemon zest**

⅛ teaspoon **cayenne pepper**

2 tablespoons **extra-virgin olive oil** or
 unsalted **ghee**

In a small bowl, combine the bread crumbs, parsley, garlic, lemon zest, cayenne, and olive oil and mix until full incorporated. Store in an airtight container at room temperature for up to 1 week.

SALSA VERDE ENCHILADAS
with COCONUT CREMA

.... *Serves 4*

Enchiladas makes us think of weeknight family meals. It's simple, a dinner in one dish, and such a crowd pleaser. Shredded chicken mixed with Salsa Verde is the filling of these crispy enchiladas. Before baking them in the oven, we add a hearty drizzle of our vegan cheese sauce and finish it with coconut yogurt and plenty of cilantro. Gooey, crunchy, and deliciously filling! (We like the turmeric tortillas best for this recipe.)

2 pounds bone-in **chicken thighs** or breasts

1 small **white onion**, cut in half

4 **garlic** cloves

1 tablespoon **Himalayan pink salt**

½ cup **avocado oil**

4 recipes **Rainbow Tortillas** (page 39) or store-bought grain-free **tortillas**

2 cups **Salsa Verde** (page 151) or store-bought

½ cup **vegan cheese sauce**, homemade (see page 44) or store-bought

1 cup crumbled **dairy-free feta cheese**, homemade (see page 46) or store-bought

1 cup **coconut yogurt**, homemade (see page 26) or store-bought

Chopped onion, for serving (optional)

¼ cup **chopped cilantro**, for garnish

Note

You can also shred the meat from a leftover or store-bought roast chicken.

1. Preheat the oven to 450°F.

2. Place the chicken, onion, garlic, and salt in a large saucepan and add water to cover by 1 inch. Bring the water to a boil over high heat, then reduce the heat to medium and simmer until the chicken is cooked through, 20 to 25 minutes.

3. Transfer the chicken to a cutting board and let cool, reserving the stock for another use. Shred the meat using two forks, discarding the skin and bones.

4. Heat the avocado oil in a medium skillet over medium-high heat. When the oil is shimmering, working quickly, add the tortillas, one at a time, and cook for about 10 seconds per side, until soft and lightly browned. Set aside on a wire rack or baking sheet. Add more oil between batches, if needed.

5. Reduce temperature to 350°F. To assemble, spread ½ cup of the salsa in the bottom of a 9 × 13-inch baking dish. Place 2 to 3 tablespoons of shredded chicken on each tortilla, top each with 1 teaspoon of the salsa, roll up, and place seam side down in the baking dish. Pour the remaining salsa and the vegan cheese sauce over the rolled tortillas and sprinkle with about half of the crumbled feta cheese. Transfer to the oven and bake until the sauce is bubbling and the cheese is melted, about 15 minutes.

6. In a small bowl, combine the coconut yogurt and ¼ cup water and stir until fully incorporated.

7. To serve, dollop with the coconut crema and sprinkle with the remaining feta and, if desired, the chopped onion and cilantro.

POLENTA BOARD

On our first trip to New York together, it was the middle of winter and we had our husbands and newborns in tow. The weather was pretty miserable, so the warm and cozy corner of an Italian restaurant was exactly what we needed. At Sauce, on the Lower East Side, a waiter emerged with what he called "the plank." He generously poured warm polenta over it, topped it with a rich ragù, and finished it with a drizzle of olive oil. It was pure heaven. This is our version of that dish. If you don't have a wooden plank at home, you can still impress your friends by pouring the polenta into a shallow serving bowl or rimmed plate. It's perfect on a cold day when you need to fill your home with warm, golden cooking smells. Sometimes the only cure for the winter blues is a bowl of something wonderful.

3 cups **almond milk**, homemade (see page 26) or store-bought

½ teaspoon **ground turmeric**

1 teaspoon **honey**

2⅔ cups **almond flour**

2 tablespoons **flax meal**

½ teaspoon **minced garlic**

Himalayan pink salt and freshly ground **black pepper**

3 cups **Bolognese** (page 261)

2 tablespoons **olive oil**, for drizzling

¼ cup **basil**, chiffonade

1. In a small saucepan, combine the almond milk, turmeric, and honey and bring to a boil over medium low heat. Slowly stir in the almond flour and flax meal, whisking continuously to prevent lumps. Reduce the heat to low and cook for 5 minutes, whisking continuously, until bubbling and thickened. Add the garlic and season with salt and pepper. The texture should be velvety and quite thick, not soupy.

2. To serve, pour the hot polenta in the middle of a medium wooden plank or serving dish and top with the hot Bolognese, a drizzle of olive oil, and a sprinkle of basil. Enjoy immediately.

Notes

This method of cooking works best on steaks that are at least an inch thick. For thinner cuts of beef, pan searing is a more effective method.

You don't have to dry the steak out overnight, but the dryer your steak is, the better caramelization you'll get on the meat.

ROASTED STEAK
with LOADED SWEET POTATOES AND POPOVERS

Steakhouse dinners are as much about the sides as the main course. A thick, perfectly cooked steak (our method gets the best medium-rare every time) with Claire's Thanksgiving Popovers and our version of the classic baked potato—the loaded sweet potato—is the best steak dinner you can get without trekking to a restaurant. The loaded sweet potatoes can be enjoyed on their own as a hearty lunch, but they're especially good alongside this juicy steak.

FOR THE STEAK

4 (1-inch-thick) **steaks** (we like rib eye)

½ teaspoon **garlic powder**

½ teaspoon **Himalayan pink salt**

½ teaspoon **freshly ground black pepper**

1 tablespoon **avocado oil**

1 tablespoon **unsalted ghee**

FOR THE SWEET POTATOES

4 **sweet potatoes** or **yams**

Himalayan pink salt and **freshly ground black pepper**

OPTIONAL TOPPINGS

4 tablespoons **unsalted ghee**

4 slices **bacon**, cooked until crisp, coarsely chopped

4 tablespoons **coconut yogurt**, homemade (see page 26) or store-bought

4 tablespoons **dairy-free feta**, homemade (see page 46) or store-bought

2 tablespoons finely chopped fresh **chives**

2 tablespoons **scallions**, green and white parts thinly sliced

1. Generously season the steak with garlic powder, salt, and pepper, then place them on a metal rack fitted on a baking sheet. Refrigerate at least 4 hours and up to overnight uncovered.

2. Make the sweet potatoes. Preheat the oven to 425°F. Line a separate baking sheet with parchment paper.

3. Prick the sweet potatoes all over with a fork, then place them on the prepared baking sheet and bake until tender, 45 to 50 minutes. Remove the potatoes from the oven and reduce the oven temperature to 225°F.

4. Let the potatoes cool for 10 to 15 minutes.

5. Meanwhile, make the steaks. Place the baking sheet with the steaks in the oven and cook for 25 to 30 minutes, until a meat thermometer inserted into the center of the steak reads 125° to 130°F, for medium-rare. Remove the steaks from the oven.

6. Heat the avocado oil in medium heavy-bottom skillet over high heat. When the oil starts smoking, transfer the steaks to the skillet along with the ghee and sear, press down with a spatula, about 45 seconds per side, until dark and crisp. Take the potatoes and slice down the center and top with ghee, bacon, coconut yogurt, feta, chives, and scallions, if desired.

7. Serve the steaks immediately with the loaded sweet potatoes and popovers (see page 79).

RACK OF LAMB
with ROASTED SWEET POTATOES

We each have our own connection to this recipe. For Laurel, Greek Easter is all about the lamb—it's at the peak of the season, and the rack is a centerpiece, like a turkey at Thanksgiving. For Claire, lamb chops with minted peas were her nana's go-to whenever she visited. In this presentation, lamb becomes an event. It's the one your friends will tell their friends about. The one your mom will compliment you on. This is the pull out all the stops, don't hold back, do All the Things recipe. With a heavy dose of garlic, rosemary, and lemon, we love it served over roasted sweet potatoes. The caramelized sweetness is delicious with the earthy, savory flavors from the lamb. The meal is made even better with our Fresh and Bright Tzatziki (page 147) drizzled on top.

4 medium sweet potatoes, cut into 1½-inch cubes (we prefer Japanese sweet potatoes with white flesh)

½ cup plus 2 tablespoons avocado oil

1 tablespoon cider vinegar

1 tablespoon Italian seasoning

Himalayan pink salt

12 garlic cloves

4 sprigs fresh rosemary

4 sprigs fresh thyme

Juice of 2 lemons

4 racks of lamb (about 2 pounds each, 8 pounds total)

1. Preheat the oven to 450°F. Line a baking sheet with parchment paper.

2. In a medium bowl, combine the potatoes, 2 tablespoons avocado oil, the vinegar, Italian seasoning, and ½ teaspoon salt and toss to coat.

3. In a food processor, combine the garlic, rosemary, thyme, lemon juice, ½ cup avocado oil, and 1½ tablespoons salt and pulse for 1 to 2 minutes, until the mixture is evenly blended. Rub the mixture all over the lamb and place on the prepared baking sheet, with the curve of the rack facing down. Surround the lamb with sweet potatoes and bake for 45 minutes to 1 hour, until a meat thermometer inserted into the thickest part of the lamb reads 165°F for medium-rare.

4. Serve each rack of lamb over the sweet potatoes and enjoy.

FISH AND CHIPS PUB FRY

.... *Serves 4*

We love the beautiful days so common in England's countryside, and the gorgeous architecture of busy London—but mostly, Laurel is obsessed with Kate Middleton. Her secret dream (whoops—not a secret anymore, we guess!) is to bake a cake with Kate and Wills, Mary Berry–style, and for her son Nico and Prince George to be playmates. They already have matching knee socks! To honor her love for our neighbors across the pond, we created an anti-inflammatory version of the country's classic fish and chips. Arrowroot acts as the agent for crisping the fish to perfection in this recipe, and the paprika helps bring a hearty, layered flavor to the batter.

FOR THE CHIPS

1 pound white **sweet potatoes**, peeled and cut into large wedges

1 teaspoon **garlic powder**

1 tablespoon **nutritional yeast**

1 teaspoon **smoked paprika**

1 teaspoon **Himalayan pink salt**

3 tablespoons **avocado oil**

1 tablespoon **cider vinegar**

FOR THE FISH

¾ cup **arrowroot powder**

1 tablespoon **almond flour**

1 tablespoon **coconut flour**

1 teaspoon **smoked paprika**

1 teaspoon **Himalayan pink salt**

2 **large eggs**, lightly beaten

¼ cup **coconut milk** or **almond milk**

2 pounds **cod**, cut into 3-inch strips

Avocado oil, for frying

Mayonnaise, homemade (see page 29) or store-bought, for serving

Cider vinegar, for serving

1. Preheat the oven to 450°F. Line a baking sheet with parchment paper.

2. Make the chips. In a large bowl, combine the potatoes, garlic powder, nutritional yeast, paprika, and salt. Add the avocado oil and vinegar and toss to coat. Place on the prepared baking sheet and bake for 45 minutes to 1 hour, until golden brown and crispy on the outside but tender in the middle.

3. Meanwhile, make the fish. In a separate large bowl, combine the arrowroot, almond flour, coconut flour, paprika, and salt, then stir in the eggs and milk. Working with one piece at a time, dredge the fish in the flour mixture, shaking off any excess.

4. Heat 1 inch of avocado oil in a medium skillet over medium heat. When the oil is shimmering, working in batches, add a few pieces of dredged fish to the skillet and cook for 2 to 4 minutes per side.

5. Plate the fish with the chips. Serve with mayonnaise for dipping and cider vinegar to add bite.

LASAGNA BOLOGNESE
with NO-BREAD BREAD CRUMBS

Serves 6 to 8

Laurel is the kind of person to stock your fridge with easy-to-reheat meals when you're sick or to show up on your doorstep after a hard day with a tray of something warm. It's almost a shame she missed out on midwestern casserole culture, having been born out west! Her meal offerings would've fit right into a church basement next to tamale pie and noodle casserole, food made with love and with a mission to comfort. Our lasagna is exactly that. We have classic meat sauce that you'll want to make extra of to keep in the freezer—it's the perfect last-minute topping on roasted sweet potatoes or cauliflower rice for an easy dinner. These simple flavors transform as they slowly cook together and are even better when reheated the next day.

Basic Pasta Dough (page 37), rolled out and cut into 3-inch-wide noodles

6 cups Bolognese (recipe follows)

1 cup dairy-free sliced mozzarella, homemade (see page 47) or store-bought

½ cup chopped fresh basil

1½ cups grain-free bread crumbs, homemade (see page 34) or store-bought

1. Preheat the oven to 375°F.

2. In a 9 × 13-inch baking dish, add a layer of noodles, barely overlapping. Add 2 cups of the sauce, ¼ cup of the mozzarella, and a third of the basil. Repeat with the remaining ingredients, then finish with the remaining ¼ cup mozzarella on top.

3. Top with the bread crumbs and bake for 25 minutes, or until bubbling. Turn the oven to broil and cook for 5 minutes more, or until the bread crumbs are browned and crunchy. Remove from the oven and let cool for about 20 minutes before serving.

4. Cover with aluminum foil and store in the fridge for up to 1 week or in the freezer for up to 3 months. Reheat in the oven.

BOLOGNESE

Makes 6 cups

¼ cup **unsalted ghee**

3 tablespoons **extra-virgin olive oil**

1 large **yellow onion**, finely diced

¾ cup finely diced **carrot**

¾ cup finely diced **celery stalk**

4 **garlic cloves**, minced

1 teaspoon **Himalayan pink salt**, plus more to taste

1 pound ground **beef chuck** (beef shoulder, 80% lean)

1 pound ground **pork shoulder**

¼ cup diced **sugar- and nitrate-free pancetta** or **bacon**

¾ cup **beef broth**

¾ cup **almond milk**, homemade (see page 26) or store-bought or **cashew milk**

1 (28-ounce) can diced **tomatoes**

Freshly ground black pepper

1. Melt the ghee and olive oil together in a large saucepan over medium heat. Add the onion, carrot, celery, garlic, and salt and sauté for 5 minutes, stirring frequently, until translucent. Increase the heat to high and, working in batches, if necessary, add the beef, pork, and pancetta; do not overcrowd the pan. Cook, breaking it up with a wooden spoon, until seared golden brown all over, 15 to 20 minutes. Reduce the heat to medium and cook for about 15 minutes more, until thoroughly browned.

2. Add the broth to the browned meat and vegetables and cook for 2 to 3 minutes, scraping up the browned bits with a wooden spoon. Add the milk, diced tomatoes, salt as needed, and pepper. Bring to a boil, then reduce the heat to low and let simmer, half covered, for 2 hours, stirring occasionally, until thick.

ACKNOWLEDGMENTS

To the Clarkson Potter team, Laurel and I consider ourselves so fortunate to have you behind us. Thank you for letting us feel like we could take chances and create a cookbook from the heart. You've all been so attentive and collaborative, we couldn't imagine a better team to guide us through creating our cookbook. Alison Fargis, you've been such a fabulous advocate for us from the beginning, and thank you for having our backs every step of the way. You've helped us up our learning curve and encouraged us to create the book we have hoped for since our first phone call, thank you!

Laurel

Thank you to my husband, Nick, for encouraging me, supporting me, loving me throughout my entire journey at Sweet Laurel, and before. My boys, Nico and Cal, for being the biggest sweethearts, filled with joy, and for being so patient while mom tends to their big sis, Sweet Laurel. I love you dearly. My mom and dad and all my brothers and sisters (and their partners!) for being taste testers for as long as I can remember and inspiring me early on to experiment with cooking and baking (and to use alternative and healthy ingredients). This includes my parents- and siblings-in-law! Your encouragement and love are endless. I love you right back. Elsie and Patty, thank you for all your care for my children, and being my right hand at home while I'm working. Endless thank yous to all of our team members at Sweet Laurel who make it possible to bring decadent and nourishing food to people around the world. And to my talented and beautiful friend Claire, thank you for being my extraordinary visionary and partner at Sweet Laurel. Your big picture perspective and eye for beauty, branding, and design are an invaluable asset at Sweet Laurel.

Claire

Thank you to my family—this book is filled with recipes inspired by the Sunday dinners we've shared, from Mum's pasties to Dad's steak and French fries. Our love of food has shaped me, and now this book—thank you for your taste testing, encouragement, and love. And a special kiss to my boys, Craig and James. Thank you for all of the dishes you've washed, hugs you've given, and especially for the "I love yous."

INDEX

Published in the United States by Clarkson Potter/Publishers, an imprint of
Random House, a division of Penguin Random House LLC, New York.
clarksonpotter.com

CLARKSON POTTER is a trademark and POTTER with colophon is a
registered trademark of Penguin Random House LLC.

Library of Congress Cataloging-in-Publication Data has been applied for.

ISBN 978-1-9848-2555-1
Ebook ISBN 978-1-9848-2556-8

Printed in Malaysia

Food Photography: Claire Thomas
Food Styling: Claire Thomas
Lifestyle Photography: Elsie Dardon
Prop Styling: Kate Martindale
Recipe Testers: Danielle Daitch, Shanna Scott, Jenn Knight

Editors: Amanda Englander and Lydia O'Brien
Designer: Mia Johnson
Production Editor: Joyce Wong
Production Manager: Kim Tyner
Marketing: Brianne Sperber
Publicity: Natalie Yera
Composition: Merri Ann Morrell, Hannah Hunt
Copy Editor: Ivy McFadden
Indexer: Elizabeth T. Parson

10 9 8 7 6 5 4 3 2 1

First Edition